MEDIEVAL
FLOWERS

MIRANDA INNES & CLAY PERRY

MEDIEVAL
FLOWERS

MIRANDA INNES & CLAY PERRY

KYLE CATHIE LIMITED

First published in paperback in Great Britain 2002 by
Kyle Cathie Limited
122 Arlington Road, London NW1 7HP
general.enquiries@kyle-cathie.com
www.kylecathie.com

First published in hardback in 1997 by
Kyle Cathie Limited

ISBN 1 85626 418 1

A Cataloguing in Publication record for this title is
available from the British Library

Designed by Sarah Perry

Printed and bound in Spain by Artes Gráficas Toledo S.A.U.
D.L. TO: 1013 - 2002

HALF-TITLE PAGE: **Detail from a 16th-century
Flemish *Hours of the Virgin*.**
PAGE 2: **Peony (*Paeonia mascula*).**
TITLE PAGE: **Peony (*Paeonia officinalis*).**
CONTENTS PAGE: **Dog rose (*Rosa canina*).**

Contents

Foreword

My passion for medieval flowers began some years ago when I was working with Mary Keen on *The Glory of the English Garden*. The work on this book took me to Queen Eleanor's Garden in Winchester, which is a reconstruction of an authentic medieval garden. I became absorbed by the quiet simplicity of the place, and after spending some time working in the garden, I became aware of the qualities of the plants, and how few there were compared to the modern gardens to which I am accustomed. Most of the plants were primarily used for their medicinal and culinary properties, and many were imbued with symbolic and magical qualities at a time when the perception of spiritual matters was quite different to our own.

I was drawn in to the medieval world once again when I illustrated Candace Bahouth's *Medieval Needlepoint*, for which I spent a lot of time leafing through books of medieval illustrations, illuminated manuscripts and the *Book of Hours*. These Flemish masterpieces had in the margins extravagantly beautiful motifs of individual blooms and insects on gold backgrounds – giving them a quite jewel-like quality. It was these and the Mille Fleurs tapestry in the Cluny Museum in Paris that were the main inspiration for the book.

The plants, so lovingly depicted in the ancient records, became a tantalizingly limited indication of what could be possible to photograph. It was not until some time later that I came upon the work of the horticultural scholar John Harvey, to whom I am deeply indebted: his Medieval Gardens is essential to anyone interested in the subject. Harvey's definitive list of all the flowers and plants that were known in the Middle Ages from the time of Charlemagne was invaluable in the realization of this book.

It was impossible to photograph all the plants in the list, so I have done my best to present the most beautiful and well-loved flowers and herbs. This book does not aim to be an academic treatise, but rather attempts to celebrate the qualities of these ancient inhabitants of our gardens in that hope that it will inspire the creation of many a new paradise garden, or an appreciation of a more contemplative time.

In the interests of authenticity, I have tried to avoid hybrids (though this has not always been possible) and I have omitted anything that was introduced into Europe after 1500 – the beginning of the Tudor period.

Clay Perry, May 1997

The iris (*Iris germanica*) has been cultivated for longer than almost any other decorative plant.

The Labours of the Months, a 15th-century German
painting showing a couple busy in an orchard with
scythe and rake.

Introduction

Medieval gardens are where the healing arts, poetry, spirituality, a sense of order in the cosmos and an appreciation of beauty took root and were cultivated. It is difficult to overestimate the importance of the annual cycle of blossom and fruition in the Middle Ages. For most people, plants were the calendar by which they judged the passing of the seasons. Plants were symbols, talismans, charms, and a surprisingly rich source of fear and amusement. The extraordinary diversity of descriptive, bawdy and mystical names for common plants attests to their central role in the culture of the time.

Understandably, few people are familiar with the patterns of life and events that took place during the Middle Ages – a mysterious and unsignposted time that spans the appearance of Halley's Comet and William of Normandy becoming king of England in 1066, to the spread of the Renaissance throughout Europe, with the Tudors firmly enthroned in 1500.

The first crusade, instigated by Pope Urban II to protect pilgrims to Jerusalem, met a bloody end in 1096, and was followed by four more, one of which was the heartrending Children's Crusade in 1212, when thousands of French and German women and children starved crossing the Alps, and the survivors were sold into slavery. The glorious iconography of heraldry blazed to life in 1129 when Henry 1 presented Geoffrey of Anjou with a shield bearing golden lions. Bacon may have invented gunpowder, and thereafter it was a small step to making guns and cannons. The sorry route of depersonalized and distanced battles had begun.

In 1332 the Black Death started its inexorable progress, taking 17 years to reach England, and then killing one-third of the population in a single year despite herbal nostrums and optimistic fumigation with aromatic woods. Between 1347 and 1351 75,000,000 people died around the world. The Statute of Labourers was hastily put together in 1350 to stop peasants taking advantage of the dearth of workers by demanding high wages.

Paper began to be manufactured in the Middle Ages, allowing information eventually to be disseminated among the general population. Linen was first grown and woven in 1253. Secular music was developed with the introduction of new musical instruments – the dulcimer in 1400, the sackbut in 1495, and the virginals and viols in 1500 on the cusp of the Renaissance. Christmas carols were sung for the first time around 1210, and 'Sumer is icumen in', an early English round, was first documented in 1225. Minstrels and troubadours travelled from court to court relating the events of the day, and formed a loose alliance of undependable newscasters whose information filtered eventually to ordinary people in towns and villages.

Printing began in Europe in 1425, and in 1454 Johann Gutenburg began printing, using movable copper type – a great advance which first made books affordable for any but the aristocracy and the outrageously wealthy clergy. In 1500 Wynkyn de Worde set up a printing press in London. The jewel in his printing career was the comprehensive *De Proprietatibus Rerum* by Bartholomaeus Anglicus, a Minorite theologian, who was the only medieval Englishman to write a herbal, and whose observations about plants and flowers are as fresh and perceptive today as in the thirteenth century when they were written. The frontispiece woodcut was the first botanical illustration to be printed in an English book – the paper too was the first to be manufactured for the press.

This resume sets the broad historical scene – of direct relevance to the subject of medieval flowers and plants are the books and manuscripts which chronicled everyday life and the advances of medicine: Dioscorides' *De Materia Medica* was translated into Arabic and embellished with exquisitely detailed Islamic miniatures in 1224, and the information it

contained spread inexorably among religious and lay medical men. In 1250, Walter of Henley tackled the problems of farming in Hosebondrie which became an essential treatise. Rufinus published his fine *Herbal* shortly afterwards, and Matthaeus Sylvaticus produced a dictionary of medical herbs, *Pandectae*. In 1327, Jean Pucelle illustrated a bible with the first realistic flowers, animals and birds.

Of direct impact on gardens and what could be made to thrive was the fact that from 1150 to 1300 Europe enjoyed 150 years of comparative warmth, which fostered vineyards and a handful of unusually exotic plants. Gardens became outdoor rooms, where wooded groves, vine-shaded arbours and rose-mantled bowers were enjoyed for eating, drinking, reading, music and flirtation. From 1300 onwards, the temperature plummeted which discouraged gardeners and outdoor pursuits generally. Europe was gripped by famine in 1315.

Most of the gardening tools we use today had surprisingly similar medieval counterparts – the wheelbarrow first appears in the late twelfth century, adding muscle to the existing repertoire of ladders, axes, saws, sieves, iron forks, seed-baskets and bags, mallets, trowels, shears, scythes, sickles, spades, shovels and rakes. The number of available plant species increased dramatically during the Middle Ages – from around 100 at the turn of the millenium, to three times as many by the beginning of the Renaissance.

The art of the garden and its contents were recorded by various herbalists, encyclopedists, authors and painters. Charlemagne drew up a list of the plants to be grown in his vast empire around 800, called *Capitulare de Villis* or decree concerning towns. He required that his lands in every city should produce all the 73 herbs among which roses and lilies, dedicated to the Virgin Mary, had pride of place, and the 16 fruit and nut trees. Caper spurge, clary, flag irises, houseleek, mallows, poppies, rosemary, rue, sage and tansy were also represented. Aelfric provides another starting point in 995 – listing the Anglo-Saxon essentials. *De Viribus Herbarum* of Macer Floridus, probably written in the eleventh century, is devoted to the discussion of 80 herbs. It was translated into English in 1395, and was the first herbal to be printed, in 1477. Abbess Hildegard of Bingen (1098–1179) compiled a list of known plants, many of which were purely decorative. Alexander Neckam (1157–1217), foster-brother of Richard Coeur de Lion, followed suit, with evocative descriptions of places as well as plants in his *De Naturis Rerum*. He advocated gardens for pleasure as well as utility, which was precisely in keeping with the new fascination for courtly love. Bartholomew de Glanville, also known as Bartholomaeus Anglicus or Bartholomew the Englishman (*c*1200–1260) wrote a complete encyclopedia, of which the 17th book addresses available plants. Albertus Magnus (*c*1206–1280) was the next authority on the subject in *On Vegetables and Plants*, about which he waxed lyrical. Pietro de' Crescenzi (1230–1320) copied him, taking material from ancient history as well, and added his own observations, including guidelines for the middle-class gardener (*mediocrium personarum*) with just over half an acre to plant. The *Agnus Castus* was a Latin herbal written by an Englishman, translated into English around 1440. Henry Daniel listed medicinal plants, and wrote a treatise on the virtues of rosemary for Queen Philippa in 1338 – and started a rampant passion for the all-healing plant. He apparently grew 252 different herbs in his own garden, including an exotic novelty – the wallflower.

In this barely imaginable time, medieval gardens provided food and medicine, amusement and beauty. When war and plague confounded and frightened the population they sought solace and cure in their plants. When peace and plenty reigned, people celebrated their tapestry of flowers in painting and song. Ordinary people did not travel far, and their villages, homes and gardens were all the world they knew.

With no newspapers, no radio or television, people made what sense they could of world events and the vagaries of climate and crop. A dark undertow of superstition required lingering pagan deities to be befriended and appeased with festivals and feast-days, rituals and penances. The Catholic Church had license to indulge in despotic meddling, as did anyone else who could immure themselves behind title, money, land or power. Life was hard and nature was ruthless, weeding out the sick, the infirm and the feeble.

But people have always had an indomitable instinct for finding joy, and gardens must have been one of the unfailing resources, one of the few important pleasures, and a way to mark the passage of time when calendars and clocks were not in common use. Births, weddings and deaths were commemorated by the flowers that were in bloom at the time. Spring had arrived when leaves and buds swelled on the trees. Summer meant the grateful annual liberation from smoke-filled hovel into a larger, brighter world.

Gardens of one sort or another were a vital source of food and flavourings, medicine and pleasure to nobility, clergy and peasant. They were a potent fund of poetic imagery, and a haven from marauding beasts – pigs in particular were wont to ramble, boisterous and omnivorous, along village highways.

Most people had a garden of some kind – according to the *Domesday Book* in 1086 over 90 per cent lived in the country and off the land. Over half were 'villani', 'free men' or 'sokemen' and held 65 per cent of all land. 'Bordars' or 'cottars' had a mere 5 per cent between them. Only the slaves, just 9 per cent of the population, held no land.

For most, the garden consisted of the unvarying culinary basics – the ubiquitous cabbages, leeks, garlic, onions, together with the essential peas and beans which formed the staple diet. There would have been a waste recycling unit in porcine form rootling beneath the trees, and probably hens or geese.

But there was no distinct line drawn between utilitarian plants and decorative ones. Parsley and potherbs, which included marigolds and many other flowers, alleviated the stolid ranks, and cherries, apples and pears brought a shower of welcome blossom in spring. Most flowers did double-duty, and were treasured for their beauty as they were cultivated for their usefulness. If you do not happen to have access to paintings, tapestries, fine glass or jewels, nature provides a generous canvas upon which to feast your eyes, as lyrical poets have observed and celebrated from the Song of Solomon onwards.

There were three kinds of medieval gardeners, who produced very different gardens. There were the monks, whose gardens were mostly utilitarian, formal, and with a particular emphasis on medicinal plants. There were the rich who prospered on the labour of others – the charming hortus deliciarum depicted in painted manuscripts was their outdoor playground in which they indulged in music, endless garland-making, romance and courtly love. And there were the cottage-dwellers, whose all-purpose gardens provided food, elementary medicines, and an agreeable pastime, and for which there is unfortunately little documentary evidence. In towns, people might have access to large allotments in which to grow more mundane vegetables, keeping their gardens for the more decorative flowers, fruit and herbs.

Few medieval plants were grown for their beauty alone, almost every flower had some other use, if only that of making a scented carpet to discourage insects and help mask the oppressive odours which were a normal adjunct to everyday life without plumbing and convenient waste disposal. Alexander Neckam's

De Naturis Rerum, written in the second half of the twelfth century, makes one of the first mentions of plants as simple garden adornment. His list, is the first to commend borage and daffodils, along with the familiar roses, lilies, violets and mandrake.

Flowers formed part of the culinary repertoire, they were used medicinally, and made into salves, dyes, cosmetics and oils. They were the poor woman's jewels, they were given as gifts and love-tokens, they were threaded into garlands, they were used to decorate king's palace and cottage alike, and every festival, feast or funeral had its floral livery.

In the horticultural hierarchy, roses and lilies – emblems of Mary the mother of Christ – had precedence. Entire gardens, rosaries, were devoted to powerfully scented red and white roses and rosary beads were made of compressed rose petals. Red roses further symbolized the blood of martyrs. Fragrance was revered as the breath of God on earth, so a rose garden was doubly sacred. The roses that were likely to be lending their sweetness to these gardens of delight would be the bright red *Rosa gallica* brought to England by the Romans, *Rosa centifolia*, *Rosa moschata*, the

Snowdrops (*Galanthus nivalis*) were one of the Virgin Mary's flowers, and used to decorate lady chapels at the feast of the Purification, February 2nd.

holy rose of Abyssinia, all hedged about by the ancient *Rosa alba* which made an impenetrable scented wall. Roses also gave medieval gardeners a chance to indulge in some of their favourite horticultural practices – grafting, pruning, pollarding, pleaching, trellising, layering and shaping. Chaucer describes such a garden in the *Franklin's Tale*:

> ful of leves and of floures;
> And craft of mannes hand so curiously
> arrayed hadde this garden, trewely,
> That never was ther gardin of swich prys,
> But-if it were the verray paradys.

The inexorable annual cycle of the seasons is keenly observed and described with feeling in *Sir Gawain and the Green Knight*. Sir Gawain, glorious champion of courtly love in the late fourteenth century, gives a poignant vision of the sequence of the seasons:

> After Christmas there came the cold cheer of
>   Lent,
> When with fish and plainer fare our flesh we
>   reprove;
> But then the world's weather with winter
>   contends:

LEFT: **Primroses (*Primula vulgaris*) were welcome garden visitants, the flowers signalling winter's end.**

> The keen cold lessens, the low clouds lift;
> Fresh falls the rain in fostering showers
> On the face of the fields; flowers appear.
> The ground and the groves wear gowns of
>   green;
> Birds build their nests and blithely sing
> That solace of all sorrow with summer comes

The daffodil (*Narcissus triandrus*) grew wild in medieval times, and was smaller than modern cultivars.

> ere long.
> And blossoms day by day
> Bloom rich and rife in throng;
> Then every grove so gay
> of the greenwood rings with song.

> And then the season of summer with the soft
>   winds,
> When Zephyr sighs low over seeds and
>   shoots;
> Glad is the green plant growing abroad,
> When the dew at dawn drops from the
>   leaves,
> To get a gracious glance from the golden sun.
> But harvest with harsher winds follows hard
>   after,
> Warns him to ripen well ere winter comes;
> Drives forth the dust in the droughty seasons,
> From the face of the fields to fly high in the
>   air.
> Wroth winds in the welkin wrestle with the
>   sun,
> The leaves launch from the linden and light
>   on the ground,
> And the grass turns to grey that once grew
>   green.
> Then all ripens and rots that rose up at first,
> And so the year moves on in yesterdays many,
> And winter once more, by the world's law,
>   draws nigh.
> At Michaelmas the moon
> Hangs wintry in the sky;
> Sir Gawain girds him soon
> For travails yet to try.

Spring

WHEN IN APRIL THE SWEET
SHOWERS FALL
AND PIERCE THE DROUGHT OF
MARCH TO THE ROOT, AND ALL
THE VEINS ARE BATHED IN LIQUOR
OF SUCH POWER
AS BRINGS ABOUT THE ENGENDERING
OF THE FLOWER,
WHEN ALSO ZEPHYRUS WITH HIS
SWEET BREATH
EXHALES AN AIR IN EVERY GROVE
AND HEATH
UPON THE TENDER SHOOTS,
AND THE YOUNG SUN
HIS HALF-COURSE IN THE SIGN
OF THE RAM HAS RUN,
AND THE SMALL FOWL ARE
MAKING MELODY
THAT SLEEP AWAY THE NIGHT
WITH OPEN EYE
(SO NATURE PRICKS THEM AND
THEIR HEART ENGAGES)
THEN PEOPLE LONG TO
GO ON PILGRIMAGES. . . .
(Chaucer, the opening of the Prologue
to *The Canterbury Tales*)

PREVIOUS PAGE: **Field of daffodills**
(***Narcissus***).

Given the fetid claustrophobia of the smoky medieval mud and thatch cottage with its tiny windows, spring and the possibility of moving out of doors made the joys of nature almost intoxicatingly seductive, as a thirteenth-century poet records:

Sumer is icumen in,
Lhude sing cuccu!
Groweth sed (seed) and bloweth med
(flowers in the meadow),
And springth the wude(wood) nu:
Sing cuccu!

Before central heating, before glazed windows, when draughts and holes in the roof were part of the bracing interaction of man and nature, the seasons ruled pitilessly. When it was cold, there were no drawers full of fine thermal underwear with which to swathe shivering bodies; homespun wool, linen or hemp do not comfort chilled skin, and what warmth they impart comes through abrasion as much as anything else. In the late twentieth century, we are almost in a position to ignore the weather; we can afford to be insouciant

LEFT AND TOP: Primroses (*Primula vulgaris*) and cowslips (*Primula veris*) were both used to make wine in medieval times.

about wind and rain, or ice and snow, since we do not have to trudge for miles to collect water, or chop and transport kindling and logs for open fires. We can turn up the heating, turn on the lights and ignore the months of darkness. To the degree that medieval man suffered, so also did he celebrate. When spring came at last, when the trees burst with blossom, there was general licence and revelry, with a great sequence of feasts and festivities.

Bartholomew the Englishman, writing in 1260, expressed a timeless reaction to the new season:

Springtime is the time of gladness and of love; for in springtime everything seems glad; the earth waxes green, trees burgeon and spread, meadows bring forth flowers, the heavens shine, and everything that in winter seemed dead and withered, is renewed.

EASTER

Easter is the first great annual celebration – named after Eostre, the pagan Germanic goddess of dawn and spring, and a relic of a much more ancient and long-lasting reawakening, the vital pivot of the pre-Christian year, which was wisely and

seamlessly adapted by the church to represent the death and resurrection of Christ. Even today it is the high point of the entire Christian religious year.

In medieval times, and presumably before, Easter went on for 17 weeks, beginning at Septuagesima (the 3rd Sunday before Lent) and ending on Trinity Sunday. Easter Sunday occurs somewhere in the middle, on the first Sunday after the full moon of the spring equinox, unless the full moon is on a Sunday, in which case Easter day is the following Sunday. Services of various kinds were held in the open air, where the participants could see the end of winter and the beginning of spring all around them in green shoots and new leaves. Until the nineteenth century, people liked to believe that the sun danced for joy as it it rose on Easter morning – people would take to the hills at dawn to witness this phenomenon. There may also once have been widespread versions of the Jewish Tu b'Shevat – the New Year for Trees, when trees were planted and fruit was eaten. A vestige remains in the inaugural tree-planting to celebrate a new building, or the birth of a child.

EASTER EGGS

Other essential elements of the Easter festivities were Pace eggs (from Pasch meaning

Easter). Pace eggs were coloured with gorse or onion skins and alcohol. There were many different variations on egg-rolling and throwing, with the plain and simple symbol of fecundity and the life force at their centre. Medieval man, troubled by behaving in an enjoyably pagan manner, could reassure himself that in fact he was reverently re-enacting the miracle of the stone rolling away from Christ's tomb. In Germany, eggs are dyed green – a reminder of quickening life – on Maundy Thursday. As an anonymous poet recorded:

Pleasure it is
To here, iwis,
The birds sing;
The dere in the dale,
The shepe in the vale,
The corne springing.
God's purveance
For sustenaunce
It is for man:
Then we always
To him give praise,
And thank him than,
And thank him than.

In Greece, hard-boiled eggs are painted red for Easter Sunday and people tap them together, confirming that Christ has indeed risen from the dead. Elsewhere in Greece armfuls of wild flowers used to be picked by children to celebrate the revival of life in the short-lived carpet of colour, before the sun baked the ground hard and bare. The objective of Easter festivities – where the

ABOVE: **It took hundreds of crocuses (*Crocus sativus*) to make a pinch of saffron.**

RIGHT: **The dog violet (*Viola canina*) looks just as pretty as its scented relative.**

tradition continues today – seems to be to get drunk, have fun, and celebrate the end of Lent. Morris dances all over England consist of six dancers plus musicians, a fool, and one other character. They wear hats garlanded with flowers, rosettes or posies, ribbons and bells, and shake sticks or wave handkerchiefs. There are local flourishes: sometimes a fruit cake, representing nature's bounty, is impaled upon a sword, and the whole thing is decked with flowers. The purpose is to celebrate fertility, and it brings good luck to have a piece of the cake.

In Wales, graves are dressed with daffodils on Flowering Sunday – Palm Sunday – in a remembrance ritual known from the 15th century as Sul y Blodau. The Irish do the same on the local saint's day, making respect for the dead into a fine art, with a mossy background to flowery wreaths, surrounded by clipped evergreens.

FASTING

Spring was the time of fasting. Spring-cleaning started from the inside, and this was the time for brewing up 'spring drinks' and 'green pottages' to purge away winter ills and to revive jaded bodies with a tonic such as nettle soup, made with fresh young nettle tops, which was a good source of vitamin C. Tansy was the Easter herb, made into puddings with eggs, flour and milk and eaten on Palm Sunday and Easter Sunday. Noxious pests and parasites were always treated with violent purging brews and laxatives containing a mixture of cleavers, sage, fennel shoots, yellow iris and redcurrant leaves. Southernwood, wormwood, tansy, gentian,

pennyroyal and hops were specific herbs used for getting rid of intestinal worms – one of the hazards of medieval life.

FEASTING

After the fasting of Lent came the feasting. This is when the last of the salted meat or pork would be eaten, together with whatever fresh meat was available. The better-off would be able to feast on lamb (the traditional Paschal lamb) or suckling pig, pigs' trotters, hams and sausages. In Italy they still continue the tradition of feasting on milk-fed lamb or kid, while in France a lamb stew cooked with the first of the green vegetables is also still served. Eggs (forbidden during Lent) featured largely in festive meals at Easter, since they also represented the stone rolled away from Christ's tomb. In England they still make simnel cake, decorated with marzipan balls representing the twelve apostles; in Russia they have kulick, a tall golden cake made with eggs and eaten with paschka, a moulded cheesecake decorated with dried fruits; and in Poland they also make a cake coloured with saffron and eggs. This is when the last of the dried fruits and nuts of the previous year would be

Crab-apple blossom (*Malus sylvestris*) has a fragile, scented, mutable charm.

The elegant spathe and spadix of Lords and Ladies (*Arum maculatum*).

used up – in hot cross buns and cakes. And it would all be washed down with beer, mead, or whatever wine people had been able to make or store: such as cowslip, birch, elderflower, elderberry, haw, clary, crab-apple, rose-hip, dandelion or clover.

HERBAL DYES

As every woman knows, spring and rising sap have the curious effect of inspiring an urgent need for new clothes, though for medieval women this required rather more effort. Hemp and flax were widely grown, and along with wool constituted the fibres woven and worn by most people. Except for royalty and the nobility, people wore the same clothes day after day – freshening them by sprinkling camomile or lavender among their folds (no dry-cleaning in those days). Only on Sundays and feast days would best clothes be brought out. While no one could acquire a totally new wardrobe, the lady of the house did have the opportunity of turning to the garden and hedgerows to collect the ingredients that would brighten up her clothes.

Most of the dye plants were easily available, and worked well on scoured and cleaned wool, though flax required more extensive treatment to make the dye penetrate. The art of dyeing was part of shared and common knowedge, and the season and condition of plants was important. Lichens, for example, gave a better colour if gathered from stones rather than the bark of trees. Spring was the best time to collect new leaves, resinous bark, early flowers, and damp mosses and lichens.

The repertoire of colours was strongest on yellows and greens, using dyer's broom (yellow), camomile (yellow), tansy (mustard yellow), bracken (green-yellow), nettles (grey-green), scabious (yellow and olive green), marigold (pale yellow) and saffron (yellow). For other colours they used lady's bedstraw (coral pink), blackberry shoots (blue-grey), madder (red), onion skins (orangey brown) and elder leaves and berries (purple). Woad was the only source of blue until indigo became available. Meadowsweet roots, yellow iris flag roots and walnut shells all gave black.

'Fashion' as a notion of intended obsolescence did not become a reality until around 1350, with the flowering of courtly love and dalliance. Suddenly women took to wearing tight-laced dresses with low necklines, and fancy head-dresses. Prior to this date, women had tended to look like nuns, completely swathed in flowing shapeless garments, and covered from chin to toe.

THE SAFFRON CROCUS

Saffron was not only an important colouring for clothes, it was also used as a hair and food dye, and cost almost as much as gold. The saffron crocus – its name comes indirectly from the Arabic za-faran, meaning yellow – was prized by the Arabs for its culinary, medicinal, disinfectant and dyeing properties. Saffron came to Europe via the Moorish Empire in Spain: their eleventh-century *Book of Agriculture* explains in detail the culture of saffron. From there, the precious substance, the minute stigmas of the crocuses loaded with yellow pollen, fragrant and muskily flavoured, found its way to Germany, the Low Countries and Britain. The Arabs forbade the export of the highly-prized bulbs, but they were smuggled out of Jerusalem in the hollow walking-stick of an English pilgrim. He grew it successfully in the village that came to be known as Saffron Walden, though it took a tremendous number of plants to make just one pinch.

But saffron was greatly prized by medieval cooks for the saffron-coloured sauces and puddings, as well as making a splendid hair dye and paint for illuminating manuscripts. The laborious, time-consuming business of growing and harvesting was considered

Wild garlic (*Allium ursinum*).

LENTEN IS COME WITH LOVE TO TOUNE

WITH ALL BLOSMEN AND WITH BRIDDES

ROUNE

THAT ALL THIS BLISSE BRYNGETH.

DAYES-EYES IN THIS DALES,

NOTES SUETE OF NYHTEGALES;

UCH FOWL SONG SINGETH.

THE THRESTELCOC HIM THRETETH OO;

AWAY IS HUERE WYNTER WOO

WHEN WODEROVE SPRINGETH.

(14th-century song celebrating spring)

labour well spent. John the Gardener devotes a short verse to its care:

Forsooth, if they bear,
They should be set in the month of September,
Three days before St Mary Day nativity
Or the next week thereafter; so must it be.
With a dibble you shall him set.
That the dibble therefore be blunt and great:
Three hands deep they must set be.

WOODLANDS

Orchards and woodland gardens were much beloved of medieval man – for blossom and fruit, and for the hunting with which the nobility liked to pass their time. The poem 'De Ornatu Mundi', written in 1099, still strikes a universal chord and neatly encapsulates the thrifty medieval notion of beauty and utility combined:

There every tree a
double honour shares;
Its boughs bear fruit,
its shadow cloaks the soil:
Both are enjoyed by men,

its fruit and grateful shade.
The apple, olive, pear-tree
burgeon forth
With apples, fresh green leaves,
and ripening pears.
The chants of bird, odour of spice, and
flowers' hue
Fill air with song,
with scent the nostrils,
and adorn the soil.
Soft zephyrs waft, not harsh east wind;
perfumes transpire, not ice; there spring
not winter reigns.

Spring is the time when woodland flowers burst into life, before the leaf canopy cuts out too much light. Sunshine filtering through fresh new leaves onto a grassy floor studded with the starry, white and yellow flowers of spring has always been an enchanting sight. Hellebores and snowdrops were the earliest reminders that winter might eventually end, followed by clumps of delicate wild daffodils whose lingering presence marks the sites of long-forgotten monasteries to this day.

Primroses were harbingers of spring – their Italian name, prima verola, means first flower of spring – and they were seen as symbols of

A froth of the tiny scented white starflowers of sweet woodruff (*Galium odoratum*).

WOODS BEN WIDE PLACES WAST AND
DESOLATE YT MANY TREES GROWE IN
WTOUTE FRUYTE AND ALSO A FEW
HAUYINGE FRUYTE....THEREIN
GROWYTH HERBES, GRASSE, LEES AND
PASTURE, AND NAMELY MEDYCYNALL
HERBES IN WODES FOUDE. IN SOMER
WODES BEN BEWTYED WYTH BOWES
AND BRAUNCHES, WT HERBES AND
GRASSE....BYRDES, FOULES AND BEIN
(BEES) FLEETH TO WODE, BYRDES TO
MAKE NESTES AND BEIN TO GADRE
HONY. BYRDES TO KEPE THEMSELF
FROM FOULERS AND BEIN TO HYDE
THEMSELF TO MAKE HONYCOMBES
PREUELY IN HOLOWE TREES AND
STOCKES. ALSO WODES FOR THYKNESSE
OF TREES BEN COLDE WITH SHADOWE.
AND IN HETE OF THE SONNE WERY
WAYFARYNGE AND TRAUELYNGE MEN
HAUE LYKYNGE TO HAVE RESTE AND TO
HELE THEMSELF IN THE SHADOW.

(Anon)

**Epping Forest, a last vestige of one of the vast
medieval forests, with great wide-spreading oaks,
beeches and hollies.**

SAVE, CERTEYNLY, WHAN THAT

THE MONTH OF MAY

IS COMEN, AND THAT I HERE

THE FOULES SINGE,

AND THAT THE FLOURES GINNEN

FOR TO SPRINGE,

FARWEL MY BOOK AND MY DEVOCIOUN!

NOW HAVE I THAN SWICH

A CONDICIOUN

THAT OF ALLE THE FLOURES IN

THE MEDE,

THAN I LOVE MOST THESE

FLOURES WHITE AND REDE,

SWICHE AS MEN CALLEN DAYSIES

IN OUR TOUN.

TO HEM HAVE I SO GREET AFFECCIOUN,

AS I SEYDE ERST, WHEN COMEN

IS THE MAY,

THAN IN MY BED THER DAWETH

ME NO DAY

THAT I NAM UP, AND WALKING

IN THE MEDE

TO SEEN THIS FLOURE AGEIN THE SONNE

SPREDE,

WHAN HIT UPRYSETH ERLY

BY THE MORWE;

THAT BLISFUL SIGHTE SOFTNETH

AL MY SORWE.

(Chaucer, *The Legend of Good Women.*)

beauty and innocence. Chaucer likens the fair lady of *The Miller's Tale* to a 'PrimeRole', and they were used to decorate church altars in May, in homage to the Virgin Mary.

LUNGWORT

Another woodland plant dedicated to the Virgin Mary is lungwort – on account of the pink and blue of the flowers, and the milky drops on the leaves which have inspired alternative names, Virgin Mary's milk drops, and lady's milksile. Elsewhere, in an interesting tribute to the human passion for mythologizing, the plant is called Mary's tears, the white spots being the legacy of weeping, and the changing colour of the flowers – from pink to blue – recording her blue eyes reddened with weeping. Where this is the belief, it is considered profane to pick or uproot the plant. It was also known as Jerusalem cowslip. The name lungwort records the belief that it provided useful protection against all sorts of pulmonary complaints and lung disorders, and it was frequently used to make the pottages, hot drinks and syrups which were prescribed for chesty coughs, wheezing and shortness of breath. Since it was both extremely decorative, and offered medicinal benefits it was widely planted in gardens.

COWSLIPS

Cowslips brightened pathways with flashes of yellow. Young girls whose thoughts tended to marriage used to collect great baskets of cowslips to make into balls – fragrant playthings with which they could foretell the identity of their future husband. This involved throwing the ball – called a tissty-tossty – from one to another while calling out possible candidates' names, until it fell to the ground. This, while not absolutely infallible, was a charming and innocent way to pass the time. When exhausted by this game, the playful maidens could recover their strength by sucking the nectar from the flowers. Both cowslips and primroses were called 'cuslippes', meaning cow's breath, from Aelfric onwards. This might well be a term of approbation, but cow's breath is something of an acquired taste. Both flowers were also made into wine, which was delicious, and highly popular. Cowslip wine requires a large quantity of flowers, and since they are now so rare it is unlikely that anyone today will be able to taste this lovely wine.

TOP LEFT: **Wild garlic (*Allium ursinum*).**

RIGHT: **The 'fresh periwinkle, rich of hue' (*Vinca minor*) was an essential constituent of any respectable flowery mead.**

Of the white flowers that scattered their brightness on the woodland floor, woodruff was also used as a flavouring for alcohol. Its flowers were an essential constituent of May wine and the traditional German May Bowl punch. It also cured the resultant headache and dispelled melancholy too. The tiny starry flowers, held proud of fresh green leaf-collars, exude the irresistible clean smell of new-mown hay when dried. Woodruff, whose vernacular names all speak of the affection which it excited (ladies in the hay, lady's needlework, stargrass, sweethearts), was much loved as a strewing and laundry herb, along with melilot and meadowsweet. The common smell they share is of coumarin, a chemical which is now used for the treatment of heart problems. Woodruff garlands were used to deck and sweeten churches too. For its scent, and possibly for its efficacy against fleas and other such visitants, it was used with bracken to stuff bedding and herb pillows. The appearance of the tiny woodruff flowers meant that spring had truly arrived.

GARLIC

Less seductive in terms of fragrance, wild garlic – known as ramsies, ramsons or ramsres – had valued culinary properties. Its constellations of starry flowers still glow from many a patch of dank woodland and gloomy hedgebottom. It has a delicate and deceptive beauty, which is quite overpowered by the characteristic garlic smell. In this it is the medieval plant *par excellence*.

Condemned for the most part to a diet of pease pottage and cabbage for months at a time, people welcomed anything that relieved its stodgy monotony, and while the nobility could afford more exotic herbs and even spices and dined on vast quantities of game, the peasants had to make do with whatever they

could find. Garlic and garlic sauce (which was simply onions and garlic with vinegar) enlivened almost every medieval dish. Since everyone ate it all the time the smell was not antisocial – on the contrary, one fourteenth-century writer applauded its virtues somewhat ambiguously: 'The stench of garlic voids the stench of dunghills'. It was also beloved of Chaucer's unlovely Summoner:

> Garlic he loved, and onions too,
> and leeks,
> And drinking strong red wine
> till all was hazy.

Believed to be particularly beneficial if planted on Good Friday, garlic was reputed to be something of a cure-all. It was spread all over Europe by the Romans, for whom it was essential: for cooking, for its antiseptic properties, as a general tonic, and for the relief of chest complaints. Nettles were another Roman favourite which they brought with them to deal with circulation problems in the cold northern reaches of their empire: they used to rub their bodies with them. It is likely that some might have preferred to stick with the inevitable chilblains and forego the cure.

Another white flower with medicinal properties is Solomon's seal. The roots were highly regarded for healing wounds and knitting broken bones, and people used to make an ointment from the leaves to mend a black eye. As Gerard put it, it would take but a day or two to cure 'any bruse, blacke or blew spots gotten by fals, or womens wilfulnes, in stumbling upon their hastie husbands fists'.

OPPOSITE PAGE LEFT: **Weeding, a detail from the 14th century *Luttrell Psalter*.**

BELOW: **Heartsease (*Viola tricolor*) is one of the many medicinal plants whose traditional healing properties have been confirmed by modern science.**

POSIES AND GARLANDS

For most people now, posies and bouquets only appear at weddings and funerals, whereas, judging by medieval paintings and literature, they were once an esssential part of life, performing a symbolic, decorative and possibly medicinal function. Easter was the start of the posy season. Posies and garlands, wreaths and crowns were carried and worn to counteract the general stench of medieval life, to mark festivals and rituals of one kind or another, and to ward off plagues and other ills, a lingering reminder of which still remains in the posies carried by the Queen and clergy during the distribution of Maundy money. This goes back to the fourth century, and recalls Christ washing the disciples' feet at the Last Supper. Money was given to the needy whose feet the king or queen washed, 'kneeling down upon the cushion, in succession washed one foot of every one of the 39 women, in so many silver basins, containing warm water and sweet scented flowers.'

The essential constituents of a respectable posy were likely to include a mixture of fragrant, herbal and purely pretty flowers. Lily

LEFT: **The elegant wands of Solomon's seal (*Polygonatum multiflorum*) are festooned with shy white flowers.**

of the valley provided a waft of clean, sweet scent. It grew wild in medieval times, and was one of the flowers used to decorate Lady Chapels. It was called by some Our Lady's Tears and said to have grown where she wept. Lily of the valley is not often mentioned in medieval literature, but is prettily depicted growing in the grass beneath the Virgin's feet in paintings by Jan Van Eyck.

Other scented flowers used included wallflowers and violets. Violets were reminders of the sweetness and humility of the Virgin Mary. Bartholomew expressed their virtues thus:

> **Violet is a lytyll herb in substaunce and is better fresshe and newe than whan it is olde. And the floure thereof smelleth moost . . . And the more vertuous the floure thereof is, ye more it bendyth the heed thereof dou(n)warde. Also floures of spryngynge tyme spryngeth fyrste and sheweth somer. The lytylnes thereof in substaunce is nobly rewarded in gretnesse of sauour and of vertue.**

Gerard credited them with being an early form of aromatherapy since 'They admonish and stir up a man to that which is comely and honest'. Sweet violets were made into syrup

The milky juice of spurge (*Euphorbia*) was used to remove warts. Taken internally it could produce 'violent griping and purging, with burning heat of the throat', and even death.

SPRYNGYNGE TYME IS THE TIME OF

GLADNESSE AND

OF LOVE; FOR IN SPRYNGYNG TIME ALL

THYNGE SEMETH GLADDE; FOR THE

ERTHE WEXETH GRENE, TREES

BURGYNNE AND SPREDE, MEDOWES

BRING FORTH FLOWERS, HEVEN

SHYNETH, THE SEE RESTETH AND IS

QUYETE, FOULES SYNGE

AND MAKE THEYR NESTES,

AND AL THYNGE THAT SEMED DEED IN

WYNTER AND WIDDERED, BEN

RENEWED,

IN SPRYNGYNG TIME.

(Bartholomaeus Anglicus, *c*1260)

which was used as a mild laxative, and were also used for coughs, colds, headaches, nerves and insomnia.

ROSEMARY

Rosemary was considered particularly efficacious in an anti-plague and infection posy. In medieval times it was regarded as a wonder herb, credited with being able to cure almost anything, and serve any purpose, from being used as a toothbrush, and a fragrant but somewhat ineffective hairbrush, to flavouring wine and roast meat and soothing and calming nerves and digestion. A sprig was laid on graves to show respect and loving memory long before Shakespeare encapsulated it forever as the herb of remembrance. According to the Myddfai doctors who ran a holistic school of medicine in Wales from the sixth century onwards:

If the leaves be put beneath your pillow, you will be well protected from troublesome dreams and all mental anxiety. Used as a lotion, this herb or its oil will cure all pains in the head, and a spoonful of the herb mixed with honey

The sweet smell and rich tapestry colours of wallflowers (*Cheiranthus cheiri*) made them perfect for nosegays.

An early 15th-century 'Mary Garden', showing the Virgin surrounded by over 18 different flowers.

and melted butter cure your coughing. A fine thing it is to boil in water the leaves and flowers and to use the mixture as a face wash. Do not wipe the face afterwards, but let it dry naturally. The truth is that by regularly washing their faces in this way the wise will keep their youth until the day they die.

Such claims make the reverence accorded to rosemary absolutely comprehensible. It was also strewn on floors and hung in wardrobes to discourage insects and moths. Gerard said that 'it comforteth the cold, weak and feeble brain in a most wonderful manner'. Rosemary was carried in the handles of walking sticks during the plague, to be sniffed in the hope of avoiding infection.

DAISIES

Daisies, pinks, primroses, cowslips, lavender, rosemary, hyssop and sweet rocket were essential to a good posy. Daisies of all kinds, from the tiny meadow flowers to sizeable ox-eyes, were medieval favourites. 'As fresh as a daisy' is still a term of approval. In medieval times, when pallor and cleanliness were prized as signs of wealth and leisure, 'as white as a

Clouds of white hawthorn blossom (*Crataegus monogyna*). The musky smell is strongly evocative of spring.

daisy' was a compliment. If the posy maker grew bored, she could resort to the time-honoured pastime of 'he loves me, he loves me not' as she picked off the tiny petals, hence the name 'measure of love' for the humble daisy. Large or small, daisies were regarded fondly by medieval gardeners, who did all they could to encourage them. Indeed German medieval paintings often show gardens in which the close-cropped turf is strewn with daisies and their regular companions, dandelions. Such portrayals of the natural resurgence of life in springtime provide an arguably more realistic and emblematic portrayal of the resurgence of life come spring than the ubiquitous prim manicured herbers of French miniatures.

Posies are still sometimes carried in ceremonial processions today. They may look incongruous, even slighly ridiculous when solemnly carried by middle-aged men, but they are a relic of an ancient tradition, once considered a necessary anti-plague measure, and good for masking the redolent effluvia of life before sanitation.

Garland and posy-making was a happy and innocent pastime which must have busily occupied womens' hands in their preparations for each one of the many religious occasions of the year.

Chaucer's account of the fair Emily – personification of youthful innocence and good sense in *The Knight's Tale* – evokes the perfect image of the object of courtly devotion:

Young Emily, that fairer was of mien

Than is the lily on its stalk of green,

And fresher in her colouring that strove

With early roses in a May-time grove

– I know not which was fairer of the two –

Ere it was day, as she was wont to do,

Rose and arrayed her beauty as was right,

For May will have no sluggardry at night,

Season that pricks in every gentle heart,

Awaking it from sleep, and bids it start,

Saying, 'Arise! Do thine observance due!'.

. . . In the garden at the sun's uprising,

Hither and thither at her own devising,

She wandered gathering flowers, white

and red,

To make a subtle garland for her head,

And like an angel sang a heavenly song.

PREVIOUS PAGE: **Cow parsley (*Anthriscus sylvestris*) and campion (*Lychnis*) in a flurry of spring freshness.**

LEFT: The spotted leaves of lungwort (*Pulmonaria officinalis*) were considered to look like diseased lungs.

WREATHS AND CROWNS

The likely flowers for wreaths and crowns were pinks, snowdrops, marguerites, helichrysum, meadowsweet and campanulas. For festivals,

Its soft colours and attractive foliage has made aquilegia (*Aquilegia vulgaris*) popular for centuries.

fragrant flowers such as violets, narcissi, roses, lilies and anemones were twined into a crown. Bacchanalian processions were garlanded with twiners and climbers, such as grapevine, ivy and evergreen clematis.

SINISTER PLANTS

While the woodland contained much that was good, it was also home to the truly sinister: Lords and Ladies, for example, is a plant about which much mythology lingers. Evilly

handsome, the glossy leaves are among the first of spring. Leaves, flowers and berries produce an acrid juice which burns and causes stomach upsets. The whole plant contains an irritant which used to cause terrible blisters on the hands of the laundrymaids for whom the plant provided starch. Surprisingly, the root, once it has been well baked, becomes harmless and in this state has been used to make a drink, in the same way as arrowroot.

Once known by a variety of rude descriptive names Lords and Ladies was somewhat confusingly considered both aphrodisiac and the source of adder venom. The spots on the early unfurling leaves were reminders to the suggestible of the spots of blood beneath Christ's cross.

Spurge is another plant with an ambiguous reputation. The word spurge comes with good reason from the Latin *expurgare*, which really means to spew forth. This was Pertelote's recommended laxative for her husband in Chaucer's *Nun's Priest's Tale*:

Worms for a day or two I'll have to give

As a digestive, then your laxative.

Centaury, fumitory, caper-spurge

And hellebore will make a splendid purge;

And then there's laurel or the blackthorn

berry,

Aquilegia (*Aquilegia vulgaris*).

Ground-ivy too that makes our yard so
merry;
Peck them right up, my dear, and swallow
whole.

The acrid white sap of spurge (*Euphorbia*),
like that of dandelion, was also thought to
cure warts, callouses and carbuncles and, like
arum juice, it can certainly cause blisters. The
juice is also supposed to be effective against
rheumatism. Gerard described its virtues
with characteristic ebullience. The juice
'Cureth all roughness of the skinne,
mangines, leprie, scurffe, and running scabs,
and the white scruf of the head. It taketh
awaie all maner of wartes, knobs, and the
hard callouses of Fistulaes, hot swellings, and
Carbuncles.' As well as its medicinal
functions, caper spurge (*Euphorbia lathyris*)
had a reputation for deterring witches. And
there were more dubious uses: the irritant
properties of sun spurge sap (*Euphorbia
helioscopia*) have been used by the men of the
Isle of Man as a dubious sex aid, for which
sour milk was the antidote if the resultant
swelling and discomfort proved unendurable.

The milky juice from Irish spurge
(*Euphorbia hyberna* or *Baine caoin*) contains

**A glossy explosion of brilliant yellow must have
cheered the spirits even though it came from the
humble buttercup (*Ranunculus*).**

saponins which destroy the gill tissue of fish, so that they die and float conveniently on the surface of the water – a factor exploited by the hungry natives of Kerry and West Cork.

And life was often hard. In times of famine, people were reduced to desperate expedients just to stay alive:

> Wylde men of wodes and forestes useth that sede (birch) instede of breede (bread). And this tree hath moche soure juys and somwhat bytynge. And men useth therfore in spryngynge tyme and in harvest to slyt the ryndes and to gader ye humour that comyth oute thereof and drynkyth in stede of wyn. And such drynke quencheth thurste. But it fedyth not nother nourryssheth not, nother makyth men dronke.

Bartholomew the Englishman obviously did not rate birch juice highly, but implies the appalling deprivation suffered by these mysterious men of the woods. In fact, birch sap wine is delicious. The sap is quick and easy to collect. Take sap from mature trees in spring. Simply bore a hole in the trunk and insert a length of tubing leading down to a glass collecting bottle. Leave it overnight: you

Lily of the valley (*Convallaria majalis*).

will collect about four pints. Make the wine immediately.

THE MEDIEVAL HOUSEWIFE

Winemaking, like so many other household tasks, was considered woman's work. But as the days lengthened and the sun finally began to coax leaf buds to open, the well-organized housewife would wander out from the smoke-filled cottage in which her children were brawling on the rush-strewn earth floor, and with a sigh of relief enjoy the peace, sniff the fresh green smells of leaves unfurling and turn a grateful ear to the muttering of nesting pigeons in her enclosed all-purpose garth. With dinner in mind, she would pick a handful of chives, a generous tuft of parsley, a sprig of thyme, and a posy of satiny orange pot marigold heads with which to impart a more refined flavour to the all-too-familiar dried pease pottage, spiked though it was with lively additions of leeks, garlic, onions and rough bread.

Fruit trees, flowers, herbs and vegetables grew in tangled profusion, but she knew well enough what was what. She might glance severely at the hen which had unaccountably stopped laying, with the thought that, boiled with herbs and the last of her mustard it would make the Easter celebrations a bit

more memorable. Adding a couple of angelica leaves to her basket, to chew as a digestive after dinner (which takes place at 4 o'clock), she ponders the likelihood of being able to lay her hands on some honey to make angelica cordial. She ought to replace the rushes on the floor, which are beginning to feel a bit sticky underfoot. An aromatic mixture of mugwort, fennel, mint and wormwood would be nice, and would also keep the bugs at bay. But it is too pleasant just wandering in the sunshine. She will pull up some horseradish, which will add a bit of flavour to the pottage, and which can also be cut up fine and used to heal the cut which her husband sustained when wielding the two-edged axe rather too enthusiastically in the bramble patch. She might then walk out along the hedgerow collecting young salad leaves – salad burnet, chicory, celery, endive, sorrel, hawthorn shoots, young beech leaves and hot wild radishes for piquancy – the hotter and more pungent, the better for the jaded medieval palate. Reluctantly, she might then return to her cottage to prepare the meal, leaving the sunshine outside.

TOP: Herb Robert (*Geranium robertianum*) and cow parsley (*Anthriscus sylvestris*).

ABOVE: The daisy chain (*Bellis perennis*) is the simplest, prettiest version of the ubiquitous medieval garland.

OVERLEAF, TOP: *The Lover Attains the Rose*, illuminated by the Master of the Prayer Books.

OVERLEAF, LEFT: A simple octagonal pool of Purbeck limestone in Queen Eleanor's garden in Winchester.

QUEEN ELEANOR'S GARDEN

Named after two queens, Eleanor of Provence and Eleanor of Castile, this castle at Winchester probably combined in its three herbers the best of what was fashionable in France and Spain. In recreating it, the object was to make the kind of place in which medieval royalty might disport themselves – with a private herber in which the queen might sit upon a turf seat at an octagonal table and sip a glass of wine, lulled from the worries of state by wafts of peonies, roses and lilies; there is a Purbeck limestone fountain topped by a falcon, with a trickling rill to soothe the troubled mind. On hot days she might have wished to take refuge from the sun in the tunnel which was coolly clothed in red and white roses (York and Lancaster, *gallica* and *alba*), and white and black grape vines. A cutting of the ancient Glastonbury thorn lends a froth of blossom and dappled shade, just as a reminder of antiquity.

This day day dawes,

This gentil day day dawes,

This gentil day dawes,

And I must home gone.

This gentil day dawes,

This day day dawes,

This gentil day dawes,

And we must home gone.

In a glorious garden grene

Sawe I sitting a comly quene

Among the floures that fresh bene.

She gadered a floure and set betwene.

(Sat, in the midst)

The lily-whighte rose me thoughte I sawe,

The lily-whighte rose me thoughte I sawe,

And ever she sang:

In that garden be floures of hewe, (colour)

The gelofir gent that she well knewe;

(Gelofir, gillyflower; gent, pretty)

The floure-de-luce she did on rewe, (Fleur-de-lys; had pity on)

And said, 'The white rose is most trewe

This garden to rule by rightwys lawe.'

(righteous)

The lily-whighte rose me thought I sawe,

And ever she sang....

(Carol for three voices)

Early
summer

EVERY MAN, EXCEPT IMPEDIMENT,
WOULDE WALK INTO THE SWEETE
MEADOWS AND GREENE WOODS, THERE
TO REJOICE THEIR SPIRITS WITH THE
BEAUTY AND SAVOUR OF SWEETE
FLOWERS, AND WITH THE HARMONY OF
THE BIRDS.

(Anon)

PREVIOUS PAGE: Floral embroidery in scarlet and white, evoking pastoral idylls and everyone's rural dream.

TOP: Wild strawberry (*Fragaria vesca*).

ABOVE: *Iris germanica*.

May day, the glorious moment of unconfinement, was annually celebrated all over the country: music was played, as young men and women collected blossom with which to wreath the doors and windows of their cottages – a sweet ceremony which still marks Easter in some countries. It is not possible to overstate the jubilant liberation brought by lengthening days and appreciable warmth in medieval times. Suddenly the nobility could wander out to their elaborate and formal intimate enclosures and play chess, walk, talk, flirt, eat and drink at beautifully carved marble tables, sitting on turf benches that released a stringent head-clearing whiff of camomile or thyme when sat upon. Musicians played, fountains splashed, and ladies would make garlands for their hair.

The seasons have a benign disregard for fortune and station, and hempen homespun peasants could forsake their homes too for a glorious sojourn under the sun. Having worked at their farmed strip or on their lord's demesne, they could lounge as well as any in the bosky woodland or on their patch of grass bejewelled with pimpernel and speedwell, and sing more or less tuneful roundelays, listen to the birds, play nine men's morris, eat the odd tansy cake, drink a flagon or two of small beer or cider, and frolic with the object of their passions.

Whatever the derivation, the beginning of May has for centuries throughout Europe been celebrated with processions of people carrying trees, green branches, or flowery and leafy garlands. May Kings and Queens, decked with floral crowns, May poles and May trees of some kind, also highly decorated, are almost universal. Trees have been revered as symbols of life from earliest times, and the heart of fertility rituals – the Maypole dance – is designed to reactivate the slumbering sap. May Day is the great festival of coming summer. It is a relic of pre-Christian fertility rites, with all the attendant debauchery and drunkenness – which have today been politely discarded, leaving only the garlanded and glorified phallic symbol prettily pranced about by floral-sprigged and frilly-frocked little girls, unaware, one hopes, of the saucy business they are celebrating. Traditionally, for this ceremony the prettiest girl of the village would be crowned Queen of the May. In France, in contrast she had a more orthodox religious role – May was consecrated to the Virgin Mary, and the May Queen would be crowned in the church and lead the procession in honour of the Virgin.

The centrepiece of the festivities was

arrayed with the best of the season, in a ceremony of unabashed pagan ebullience:

They have twentie or thirtie yoke of oxen, every oxe having a sweet nosegaie of flowers tyed on the tippe of his hornes, and these oxen draw home this Maiepole, which is covered all over with flowers and hearbes, bounde rounde with strings, from the top to the bottome, and sometyme painted with variable colours. And thus beyng reared up, with handkerchiefs and flagges streamyng on the toppe, they strawe the grounde aboute, binde greene boughes aboute it, sette up Sommer haules, Bowers, and Arbours hard by it.

There is an element of fertility and fecundity in all May-day celebrations, and horns, whistles, stamping and bells were a primitive alarm clock to awaken the Sun God,

and the dormant spirits of growth and regeneration. Young men and girls went out before dawn to gather flowers and blossom with which to wreath their lovers, and

The fresh green leaves and exuberant white snowballs of the guelder rose (*Viburnum opulus*).

embellish the maypole and their homes. This tradition was quite simply a licentious mass-mating, and was understandably sniffed at

disapprovingly by puritanical onlookers past the age of revelry.

GARLANDS

Flowers were part of every festival, and medieval women made garlands with which to deck people, houses and places, as enthusiastically as women pot, paint and sew today. Life was hard work for most, and there was not a huge choice of leisure pastimes, apart from those that nature proffered. For the May festivities, everyone and everything was garlanded, and anyone who has ever sweated over a mangled daisy chain will appreciate that garland-making was a fairly labour-intensive business.

Flowers were also fashioned into crowns and headgear, wreathed about doors and windows and twined about a variety of strangely shaped symbolic disguises. Garland day is another name for May Day – and the floral

SOME TO THE WOODS AND GROVES,
SOME TO THE HILLS AND MOUNTAINS,
SOME TO ONE PLACE AND SOME TO
ANOTHER, WHERE THEY SPEND ALL THE
NIGHT IN PLEASANT PASTIMES; AND IN
THE MORNING THEY RETURN, BRINGING
WITH THEM BIRCH BOUGHS AND
BRANCHES OF TREES, TO DECK THEIR
ASSEMBLIES WITHAL . . . OF FORTIE,
THREESCORE, OR A HUNDRED MAIDS
GOING TO THE WOOD THAT NIGHT,
THERE HAVE SCARCELY THE THIRD PART
OF THEM RETURNED HOME AGAIN
UNDEFILED.

(Anon)

PREVIOUS PAGE: **Purple pompoms of unpretentious chives (*Allium schoenoprasum*).**

BELOW: **Woad (*Isatis tinctoria*), much prized for its unique blue dye, with spikes of dyer's greenweed (*Genista tinctoria*).**

confections range from a posy tied to the end of a stick, to a staff entirely entwined with flowers; great double hoops covered with blossom, to huge pyramids and bells, the size of a tall man, deluged with the produce of hedgerow and garden. Whether these rituals

The handsome blue spikes of poisonous monk's-hood (*Aconitum napellus*), also known as aconite or wolfsbane.

go back 500 years or not to medieval times, they have the air of lingering and inexplicable folk memories of some kind.

Bawdy licentiousness tends not to offend at

the present day versions of this event – diluted as so often by the tender sensibilities of the Victorians. However, the surviving rituals are still fascinating. In one English village the local children carry two garlands, one of wild flowers and one of garden flowers, to show to

The curious tufty flowers of French lavender (*Lavandula stoechas*), like hovering insects.

everyone in the village. The frames are made of wood, covered entirely in elder leaves, and punctuated by posies – of bluebells, cow parsley and primroses for the wild garland,

and fruit blossom, lilac and wallflowers for the sweetly scented cultivated garland – placed so that the stalks of each are covered by the blossoms of the next. These two rival garlands are taken to every house. The ritual used to mark the beginning of the mackerel fishing,

ANCIENT RITUALS

The idea of flower-covered beehives or church bells signified something to medieval man that has been lost, but which still satisfies a yearning to mark important changes of the seasons, and to have a riotous good time.

alcohol. No community can afford to lightly jettison the ties, however anachronistic and tenuous, that bind it.

The other loss, with the passing of all these strange activities, is a diminution of one's personal history. So many of these rituals

Filigree heads of cow parsley (*Anthriscus sylvestris*), which grows freely everywhere in airy cumuli.

and after jollifications on the beach, the garlands would be taken out to sea at sunset and offered to the waters to ensure that all went well for the fishing.

The most obvious aspect of most ancient ritual is that it binds communities together, despite sometimes separating into two or more good-heartedly competitive factions, and just about everyone has a good time, whether with or without the lubrication of

must have acted as a mnemonic, enabling the participants to distinguish this spring when the elder was flowering so early, from another ten years ago, when there was still snow on the ground. And each memory holds a web of other recollections, acting like the patches in a hand-pieced quilt, recalling this event and that person. Far from being a mad instance of utterly anachronistic and atavistic nostalgia, these feasts and festivals are how we make memories, and dignify our lives with precious milestones. We often retain memories of physical activity long after the recollection of the actual event has faded, and the one can trigger the other.

THE PURPOSE OF FLOWERS

Very rarely did the housewife of the Middle Ages – for it tended to be women who cared for gardens – grow a plant for its looks alone. To earn a place in her potager, plants had to be culinary, medicinal, attractive, scented, and have a good dose of mythology thrown in. Few passed on all counts, but the different aspects of use and meaning must have given the most humble garden something of the rich multi-layered and thought-provoking quality of a good many-themed novel.

Irises did just about everything that a good plant should do. White irises symbolized virginity and the Virgin Mary. Orris – the medieval name for the powdered violet-scented roots – is still in use in perfumery and fixes the fragrance in pot-pourris. The dried root was also used for chest complaints, and as a purgative. Ink was made from the roots and

the leaves were woven into seating, strewed floors, and thatched roofs.

Another all-purpose flower was lavender. French lavender was known as stickadove and familiar to the British for centuries, and

Iris flavescens **'Florentina', which became the emblem of that city, and one of many flowers dedicated to the Virgin Mary.**

true lavender was being grown by the mid-thirteenth century. The name comes from lavare, the Latin for to wash, and lavender has always been used as a laundry herb – imbuing bedding and clothing strewn to dry

on the bushes with its fresh anti-moth fragrance. The aromatic oil which wafted into the air on crushing made it a wonderful strewing herb. Used as a mouthwash and hair rinse it contributed a welcome whiff of sweetness, which never came amiss in this unfragrant time.

If this were not recommendation enough, lavender oil has long been used for soothing inflamed joints and muscles, preventing fainting, curing headaches, clearing the brain, and calming the nerves.

COSMETIC USES

Teeth were something of a problem in an age before dentistry and flossing; 'rotting and stinking teeth', 'cankers and worms in the teeth' and 'stinking breath' were commonplace, and not surprisingly people were driven to extreme measures. They used an alarming mixture of 'burnt roots of iris, aristologia, reeds, seashells, pumice-stones, stags horns, nitre, alum and cuttle bones, all ground together' to annihilate the problem – and the teeth too, quite possibly. If this mixture proved too difficult to find, they

RIGHT: *Emblemes et devises d'amour.*

OVERLEAF: **A decorative adjunct to water margins,** *Iris pseudacorus* **grows tall, with scrolls of yellow flowers in May and June.**

could make do with rubbing their teeth with strawberry juice to whiten them. Women could spread their faces with a mixture of chopped horseradish and milk to close their pores, and achieve a fashionable pallor with elderflower infusion. They could use a handful of calendula petals to give their hair a reddish sheen, or they might have favoured camomile or verbascum for 'golden thread' hair. Older women may have collected poppies or ivy berries with which to hide the increasing grey. If these remedies did not succeed, they could have tried sage or betony for the same purpose.

CULINARY PLANTS

The culinary plants in medieval gardens were likely to include chives with its purple pompom flowers, of which Henry Daniel said: 'It keepeth himself in ground over winter . . . we eat it as cress or porret; many say it destroyeth weak blood.' Other commonly used potherbs included trefoil, bugloss, borage, purslane, fennel, thyme, hyssop, parsley and mint. Thyme was an emblem of courage, and in the Middle Ages ladies presented their knights with 'favours' embroidered with a sprig of thyme. Horseradish was another popular flavouring, with the reputation for dealing with kidney

problems; angelica which, besides being a very handsome addition to the garden is good for heartburn and sore throats; wild strawberries which were the fruit of Venus and the Virgin Mary – and were a delectable cure for fevers, and the ubiquitous and joyous pot marigold about which Macer waxed poetical.

MEDICINAL HERBS

Flowers and herbs were not just the raw material of the decorators and garland experts. For centuries mystics and medical men were one and the same, and herbs were the magic to which they had access. In fact, until the seventeenth century, and 'chemical medicine', herbs were just about all anyone had. There were various degrees of knowledge and operating principles – the *Doctrine of Signatures* was one, which posited that the look of plants would provide clues as to their usefulness. Lungwort, with its leaves like diseased lungs, was considered to be useful for chest complaints, for example.

There were widely known and trusted cures, which everyone knew about, and the treatment plant could usually be gathered in most gardens or hedgerows. These were the

LEFT: **Graceful foliage and flowers, with a boss of golden stamens, give the peony (*Paeonia mascula*) an enduring appeal, all the better for its direct lineage to medieval gardens.**

simples (plants with a specific action) relied on by housewives for everyday coughs, sores, cuts, burns and digestive problems.

There was also the system of humours, instigated by Hippocrates and spread abroad by Galen, in which the perfect balance of blood, bile, phlegm and choler was achieved by using plants and substances that were assigned labels fairly arbitrarily as hot or cold, moist or dry. Pedanius Dioscorides, a first-century army surgeon, was one of the most influential herbalists, and with good reason – his prescriptions were based on experience and observation, and worked. His opinions were disseminated throughout Europe, and filtered in time throughout society, down to the level of common people, like the tavern-keeper's wife in *The Tale of Beryn*:

For many a herb grew for sew (pottage)
and surgery;
And all the alleys fair i-paris (trimmed), i-
railed and i-maked;
The sage and the hyssop, i-frethid (bound)
and i-staked;
And other beds by and by (full) freshly i-
dight (dressed),
For comers to the house,
right a sportful sight.

ABOVE: **A hundred ballads of a lady and her lover (15th century).**

Hyssop was used as a purge, a chest herb, a strewing herb and to flavour omelettes, pottages and pickles, while sage guaranteed long life, free of venom and pestilence. A popular proverb was: 'He that would live for aye, must eat sage in May.' Sage is antiseptic and astringent, and was used for coughs, colds, menstruation problems and liver complaints. Sage tea was used to treat sore throats, tonsillitis, mouth ulcers and infected gums. The leaves were also chewed to whiten teeth. Thyme has always been valued as an antiseptic and anti-inflammatory herb, and was also used in soaps, perfumes and pot-pourri.

MYSTERIOUS REMEDIES

There were also the more arcane, potentially dangerous, valuable or mysterious remedies, about which monastic herberers had knowledge based on their reading of antiquity, and whose formulae were generally kept secret.

Most monastic orders, the Benedictines in particular, saw caring of the sick as one of their roles, and to this end nurtured physic gardens.

PREVIOUS PAGE: **One thousand years of culture have not dimmed the exotic impact of *Paeonia officinalis* which is still a scarlet and golden star.**

LEFT: **The pink and white spires of foxglove (*Digitalis purpurea*). Foxgloves were the medieval treatment for scrofula.**

Infirmary monks might be safely assumed to know the uses and dosage of such potent but dangerous plants as the foxglove. Its alternative name, dead man's bells, has more sinister connotations and implies that the plant may have featured in the medieval poisoners' repertoire. Foolhardy or desperate patients might consent to use it as a purge or emetic. Until its importance in heart treatment was discovered in the eighteenth century, its common medical uses were more prosaic – as a cure for dandruff or a scabby head, and the leaves were made into poultices to calm headaches and inflammation.

Henbane is another valuable plant to be treated with caution. It is poisonous, though it was used as a sedative and painkiller, and it had an alarming reputation as an aphrodisiac. It was also used as a mouthwash for toothache from the time of Dioscorides onwards. Effective perhaps, if you survived the treatment. Like many dangerous plants, it was was a double-edged sword, and could protect as well as destroy.

Aconite, also known as monk's-hood or wolfbane, is about as poisonous a plant as you can get, and is unnervingly common in cottage gardens. The ground root, mixed with oils, was used as a painkiller to massage aching joints.

The Anglo-Saxons had advanced knowledge of plants and their effects – they could draw on their familiarity with 500 different plants. Their wyrtzerds (herb-yard or

Henbane (*Hyoscyamus niger*). The seeds were part of a repertoire of 'cures' used by the unscrupulous to take money from the gullible.

garden) were filled with medicinal herbs, as well as marigolds, peonies and violets. They were well versed in herbal lore, and their magical strictures for collecting herbs at certain seasons or phases of the moon are less

ridiculed now that it has been scientifically confirmed that the potency (the alkaloidal activity to be precise) of plants is affected by the time of year, the time of day and the phase of the moon. Lady Day in spring (25 March) and Michaelmas in autumn (end of September) were thought to be particularly propitious. Sunrise and sunset, using gold and hart's horn rather than iron to gather the herb, maintaining complete silence, and not looking back – these were the most common instructions for gathering herbs.

In Wales there was a rational, holistic and humane school of medicine at Myddfai in the sixth century, which continued to care for the sick and prospered until the eighteenth century. They believed, as do successful alternative healers today, that the patient was ultimately responsible for his own cure. Their treatments were the slow and sure ways of infusions and poultices, straightforward, and made up of the plants and substances that were universally familiar – milk, honey, egg white and lard were the vehicles for many of the herbs, whose effectiveness has in some cases been startlingly vindicated in laboratory tests.

The *Leech Book of Bald*, written around 900 AD (doctors were called leeches in those days) is the earliest medical book written for

ABOVE: **St George and the Dragon from a Flemish** *Book of Hours.*

RIGHT: **The dramatic black hearts of garden poppies** (*Papaver rhoeas*).

the layperson. Its recommended herbal talisman was composed of dock elder, helenium, lupin, marsh mallow, strawberry leaves, wormwood and yewberry. If Arthurian villains suffered from elves, their predecessors were cursed with 'flying venom' – a notion that was still preserved in quaint traditions centuries later. The anti-venom arsenal was composed of nine sacred herbs – atterlothe, chervil, crab apple, fennel, maythen (camomile), mugwort, stime (watercress), waybroad (plantain), wergulu (nettle). There is some overlap with the herbs which were worn as amulets and had the reputation of protecting against evil: betony, mugwort, vervain, waybroad (plantain) and yarrow. Vervain, betony and mistletoe were the Druids' most sacred herbs.

The Leech Book of Bald may have been part of the great diss-emination of medical lore promulgated by King Arthur, who wished his people to be as healthy as possible, and tried to ensure that all had access to state-of-the-art healing techniques.

With the Renaissance, herbs were superseded by more alarming chemical treatments, which as often as not, cured the ill but killed the patient. The reason, as the translator of *The Grete Herbal* diagnosed, was that there was no money to be made from dispensing herbs which everybody knew about and grew themselves, and the new breed of doctors was interested in making money. *The Grete Herbal* had the purpose of:

Enformyng how men may be holpen with grene herbs of the gardyn and wedys of the feldys as well as by costly receptes of the potycaryes (apothecaries) prepared.

Today patients still seek out the potions of 'potecaryes' and turn once more to the natural curative properties of herbs.

ABOVE LEFT: **Dyer's greenweed (*Genista tinctoria*), madder (*Rubia tinctoria*) and woad (*Isatis tinctoria*).**

RIGHT: **Marigolds (*Calendula officinalis*).**

High summer

PREVIOUS PAGE: *Rosa moschata*, the 'holy rose of Abyssinia' introduced into Europe by Christian monks.

ABOVE: *La Vie Seigneuriale*, 16th-century French tapestry.

BELOW: *Rosa* x *alba*.

Midsummer Day is dedicated to St John whose birthday it celebrates. It is one of a crop of high summer festivals whose origins go back much further than Christianity. There are lingering frissons of animal sacrifice, and much older Gods were invoked as the Druids gave thanks for another year's survival and chased away malevolent spirits, and the Romans celebrated their young. St John's Day festivities started the night before, and were a curious mixture of outright pagan sun-worship and strait-laced Christianity: as always pagans had more fun.

Midsummer is about fire and water, and there is a riddle which used to be chanted as the celebrants, wreathed with birch leaves, circled a bonfire clockwise, echoing the course of the sun through the heavens:

Green is gold.

Fire is wet.

Fortune's told.

Dragon's met.

What all this means, is that at this time of year the still burgeoning new leaves look gold in the

RIGHT: *Rosa gallica officinalis*, a neat bushy rose with fragrant flowers, also known as the 'apothecary's rose' and the 'red rose of Lancaster', and parent to the striped curiosity *versicolor*.

sunlight. The wet fire refers to a tradition whereby candles were floated on water, accompanied by a wish. If they made it to the other side, that boded well. If not, the optimistic would continue to send candle-barques across until they achieved the right result. Fishing villages would send a flotilla of torches out to sea, to ensure good catches throughout the coming year. This was one way of influencing the future.

Bonfires were part of the Midsummer repertoire, fuelled once with animal bones [bone fires] and known as Beltane Fire to the Bal-worshipping Druids. The summer solstice, July 21st, and the original date for all this sun-worship was transmuted by the church for the purposes of Christian respectability to the birthday of St John the Baptist, since it falls just three days later. But old habits die hard, and in Cornwall oak branches, wild flowers and herbs are still thrown onto the flames by a Lady of the Flowers, chanting the words:

In one bunch together bound
Flowers for burning here are found,
Both good and ill;
Thousandfold let good seed spring,
Wicked weeds, fast withering.

Lilium regale, deliciously and headily scented.

Young couples would jump hand in hand through the fire to ensure good luck. The dragon of the riddle is borrowed from St George, and has to do with a mumming play whose cast consists of a good king, a beautiful princess, an old doctor and a Red Dragon which comes to sticky end at the sword of St. George.

St John's day kept people buoyant at the end of June. This was also the favoured time for well-dressing, when flowers were used to decorate the vital sources of water by which everyone lived, and which were apt to start showing signs of drying up at this time. The plight was described in the seventeenth century thus: 'There was no Rayne fell upon the earth from the 25th day of March to the second day of May, and then there was but one shower. Two more fell between then and the 4th day of August, so that the greatest part of the land was burnt up, both corn and hay.' While this particular disaster happened later than the Middle Ages, the need to placate the spirits of the springs was no less urgent in medieval times, and the devastation caused by drought no less fearsome. August is marked by Lammas Day feasts, which are a way of giving thanks for a generous harvest. Lammas means loaf mass, and in dim recollection of Ceres and summer's bounty, fanciful loaves coloured with rose petals, saffron, plums, violets, parsley and anything else edible that came to hand, and shaped like dragons, castles, stars, moons and suns were eaten and given thanks for.

July brings St Swithin's Day with its forty days of good or bad weather and a plethora of strewing traditions, in which the floors of

churches would be covered with sedges and hay, instead of the rushes and straw which kept the chill from frozen feet in winter. The flooring material would be carried in bundles decorated with herbs and flowers to the church and presented by the village children. The girls would dress up in posy bedecked white dresses for this ceremony. In some places every pew in the church would be decorated with bunches of flowers too.

ROSES

The summer is sweeter by virtue of the lily and the rose – flowers of such overwhelming beauty that they were dedicated in the Middle Ages to the Virgin Mary, and became the measure of perfection, in comparison with which all else fell short. Poets had a field day with the rose, and made it the poignant emblem of change and mutability, of transient love and also of steadfastness, of religious devotion, purity and at the same time coldness in secular passions.

Roses have been cultivated for thousands of years, both for their fragrant beauty and their medicinal and cosmetic properties. The Chinese, the Greeks and the Romans were all wild about them. The Romans strewed rose petals in such excessive quantities at their orgies that people were known to suffocate. The oldest cultivated rose is thought to be *Rosa gallica*, the ancestor of all European medieval roses. It took the church a while to overlook such sybaritic associations, but they finally relented in true conquering fashion, by dedicating the flower to the Virgin Mary, and

ABOVE AND RIGHT: Sweet peas (*Lathyrus odoratus*) make the most fragrant nosegays, and used to be encouraged to scramble over bowers of hazel twigs, making a scented refuge from which to contemplate the world.

confecting rosary beads from fragrant compressed petals.

The conflict in the fifteenth century between the house of Lancaster (symbol: a red rose) and of York (symbol: a white rose) is still known as the Wars of the Roses. The fragrant damask rose was brought back to Europe from Persia by the Crusaders. From its petals was produced attar of roses, used for perfumes. There were many medicinal uses for roses. In Askham's Herbal there are recipes for melrosette which was honey boiled with fresh red roses: 'By the Roses he hath vertue of comfortinge and by the hony he hath vertue of clensinge.' Syrup of roses was red roses boiled with sugar and water: 'In Wynter and in Somer it maye be geuen competently to feble sicke melancoly and colorike people.' Oil of roses could be boiled, or left to macerate for four days in the sun, and rose water was dew-covered roses put in a glass and left until the sun had drawn out the colour. An early example of aromatherapy followed: 'Also drye roses put to ye nose to smell do coforte the braine and the harte and quencheth sprite.'

Rose hips contain more vitamin C than any other fruit or vegetable, four times as much as blackcurrants and 20 times as much as oranges. Gerard did not know this when he gave a recipe for rose-hip sauce for meat and fillings for tarts. However, it is likely that his medieval forbears used the fruit in a similar way, and all unknowing, suffered from a cold or two the less.

According to Bartholomew, the rose is a nonpareil: 'Among all floures of the worlde, the floure of the rose is cheyf and beeryth ye pryse. And by cause of vertues and swete smelle and savour. For by fayrnesse they fede

Scabious (*Scabiosa atropurpurea*), of which it was believed 'that the Devil did bite it for envie, because it is an herbe that hath so many goode vertues and is so benificent to mankind'.

the syghte: and playseth the smelle by odour, the touche by softe handlynge. And wythstondeth and socouryth by vertue ayenst many syknesses and euylles.' Rose honey could sort out a fit of depression like nothing else: 'Rose shreede smalle and sod in hony makyth that hony medycynable wyth gode smelle: And this comfortyeth and clenseth and defyeth gleymy humours.'

LILIES

The other great flower of the Virgin Mary was, not surprisingly, the Madonna lily. Introduced by Roman surgeons as a wound herb, Madonna lilies grew wherever there had been encampments. They eventually became emblems of the Annunciation, and were particularly associated with Our Lady of Walsingham. The venerable Bede (673 – 735) first came up with the conceit, claiming the whiteness of the petals to represent her physical purity, and the golden anthers to be the radiant light of her soul. Chaucer allies the lily very firmly with the Virgin Mary in the *Prioress's Tale* when the latter addresses Christ:

> Wherefore in honour of Thee,
> as best I can,
> Of Thee and of that whitest lily-flower
> That bare Thee, all without the
> touch of man . . .

According to tradition, the dazzling whiteness of the Madonna lily became so only after she picked one – prior to that it had been yellow. And lilies sprang up where Eve's tears fell to the ground when she and Adam were expelled from Eden. Gerard had a theory that it might be possible to colour the flowers by insinuating red, yellow or blue dye into the root, an idea that seems almost sacrilegious, given the reverence in which the Virgin's flower was held.

Lilies were given pride of place in enclosed gardens, and lent their heady glamour to Church decoration, particularly in Lady Chapels. Their strong sweet fragrance was a welcome antidote to the general pervasive rankness of human habitations. Bartholomew the Englishman describes the flower with due solemnity: 'The Lely is an herbe wyth a whyte floure. And though the levys of the floure be whyte yet wythen shyneth the lyknesse of golde.' But they were not grown solely for their spectacular flowers – the roots were considered efficacious for the treatment of boils, burns, colic and pleurisy, the petals were used to heal cuts and lily root snuff helped clear many an ale-sodden head.

POT-POURRI

Roses and lilies were important ingredients in the pot-pourri and scent balls which were used to sweeten houses, strewn among clothes and linen in chests and cupboards. Making pot-pourri is a pleasant, calming pastime, consisting of gathering petals and leaves just after the dew has dried, and stirring them into a fragrant mixture with the addition of aromatic oils, and fixatives such as orris root. Pot-pourri is still popular, using the same ingredients of rose buds, lavender, lily of the valley, pinks, lilacs, violets, meadowsweet, rosemary, woodruff, plus any herbs that appeal to you and spices such as cloves, nutmeg and cinnamon. Bay salt and powdered orris root

ABOVE: *Dianthus caryophyllus*, known as gillyflower, sops in wine, or queen of delights to the medievals. It was a great favourite for wreaths and garlands, with its aroma of cloves.

(2:1) layered between the dry ingredients will fix the fragrance. Put a lid on the mixture and leave to mature for a month or so, then moisten with rosemary oil or rosewater and mix with a wooden spoon.

Scent balls are made with the same dried pot-pourri ingredients, pounded in a pestle

THERE IS A FLOWRE WHERESO HE BE,

AND SHALL NOT YET BE NAMED FOR ME.'

'PRIMEROS, VIOLET OR FRESH DAISY?

HE PASS THEM ALL IN HIS DEGREE, THAT

BEST LIKETH ME.

ONE THAT I LOVE MOST ENTERLY.

GELOFYR GENTIL, OR ROSEMARY?

CAMAMILL, BORAGE OR SAVERY?

'NAY! CERTENLY, HERE IS NOT HE THAT

PLESETH ME.' 'I CHESE A FLOURE,

FRESHEST OF FACE.

WHAT IS HIS NAME THAT THOU CHOSEN

HAS? THE ROSE I SUPPOSE? THINE HART

UNBRACE! THAT SAME IS HE, IN HART SO

FRE, THAT BEST LIKETH ME.

(Thomas Phillipps, 16th century)

ABOVE: **Mullein (*Verbascum thapsus*).**

RIGHT: **Foaming heads of meadowsweet (*Filipendula ulmaria*) which, apart from its value as a strewing herb, has always been valued as an anti-inflammatory painkiller – the word aspirin comes from the old botanical name for meadowsweet.**

I LOVE THE ROSE, BOTH RED AND

WHITE.

IS THAT YOUR PURE PERFITE APPETITE?

TO HERE TALK OF THEM IS MY DELITE.

JOYED MAY WE BE

OUR PRINCE TO SE,

AND ROSES THRE.

NOWE HAVE WE LOVED,

AND LOVE WILL WE,

THIS FAIRE, FRESH FLOURE,

FULL OF BEAUTE.

MOST WORTHY IT IS,

AS THINKETH ME.

THAN MAY BE PROVED HERE,

ANON,

THAT WE THREE BE AGREDE IN ON.

(Thomas Phillips, 16th century)

ABOVE: **Love-in-a-mist (*Nigella damascena*).**

RIGHT: **From the time of the ancient Greeks, St John's Wort (*Hypericum perforatum*) has protected against evil spirits and demon lovers.**

and mortar with gum tragacanth and moistened with rosewater to a dough-like consistency. Shape into balls or beads to hang in cupboards, leave to harden and dry, and scent bedding and clothing with them in true medieval fashion.

THE FLOWER OF ST JOHN

St John's Wort was a tool of divination, which predicted the course of love and foretold a girl's chances of matrimony depending on whether the cut sprig wilted or remained fresh – if it remained fresh everything boded well. St John prefigured Christ, and St John's Wort, his flower, was attributed with valuable protective powers, and considered: 'A sovereign remedy against poison – even if this is due to the bite of a poisonous animal'.

Gerard distilled medieval thinking about the herb, also known as Grace of God, into a practical recipe for deep wounds, 'sinews that are pricked', or any wound made with a poisoned weapon:

Take white wine two pints, oil olive four pounds, oil of turpentine two pounds, the leaves, flowers and seeds of St Johns wort of each two great handfulls gently bruised; put them all together into a great double glass, and set

it in the sun eight or ten days; then boil them in the same glass in a bain-marie, that is in a kettle of water, with some straw in

The ragged yellow stars of elecampane (*Inula helenium*) were said to mark the trail of tears left by Helen of Troy when captured by Paris.

the bottom, wherein the glass must stand to boil. Which done, strain the liquor from the herbs, and do as you

did before, putting in the like quantity of herbs, flowers and seeds, but not any more wine.

In fact, science has corroborated Gerard's opinion, and an oil very like his secret nostrum is still used for sciatica, ulcers and sunburn.

Its power was not solely medicinal however. The balsamic smell reminiscent of incense, released from the crushed plant drove evil spirits away, raised ghosts and exorcised the undead. For magical and protective purposes, the sunbright flowers were picked drenched with dew at dawn on St John's Eve, and were smoke-dried over bonfires that evening. Then, brought to full potency, they were used for medicine or keeping evil away from hearth, home and byre, hence its ancient name *Fuga Daemonium*. It has been said of St John's Wort:

On the vigil of St John the Baptist, and on St Peter and Paul the apostles, every man's door being shadowed with green birch, long fennel, St John's wort, orpin, white lilies and suchlike, garnished upon with garlands of beautiful flowers, had also lamps of glass with oil burning in them all night . . . which made a goodly show.

In some places, wreaths of St John's Wort were hung on village houses to keep witches at bay. Wild sage was another Roman introduction. It was a essential element in monastery gardens, used both medicinally and for culinary delicacies. Sage proper was considered a sovereign cure-all:

> Why of seknesse deyeth man
> Whill sawge in gardeyn he may han.

MEDICINAL FLOWERS

Many of the high summer flowers had medicinal functions. The innocent sky-blue scabious had a variety of less than lovely applications: Gerard valued scabious highly:

> **It is called Devil's Bit of the roote (as it seemeth) that is bitten off. Old fantasticke charmers report that the Devil did bite it for envie because it is an herbe that hath so many goode vertues and is so beneficent to mankind.**

He believed that it was effective against snake-bites. Its name refers to the scab, scabies, itch or mange for which it was a cure:

> **The Decoction of the Roots taken for forty daies together, or a dram of the**

> **Powder of them taken at a time in Whey, doth (as Mathiolus saith) wonderfully help those that are troubled with running or spreading scabs, Tetters, Ring worms, yea, though they proceed from the French Pox.**

Corncockle (*Agrostemma githago*), once a pestilential problem among arable crops.

The juice was also used against the plague and to soothe plague sores. (Bryony was another cure for ring-worm, from which its alternative name, 'Tetter-berries' comes.)

Camomile had all kinds of uses – it expelled worms, acted as a mild tonic, and healed ulcers, tumours and sores when applied with a mixture of oil and vinegar. Camomile tea is still drunk by insomniacs, and it is still used as a hair rinse. In medieval times people used to scent their clothes with bunches of camomile, an important consideration before the days of dry-cleaners and washing machines.

Camomile lawns were greatly prized for their sweet apple-scented leaves that released their scent when trodden upon. Though they are quite difficult to establish, and need careful weeding and watering, the end result is a dense green fragrant mat that never needs mowing. It was credited with the ability to revive sickly plants in the vicinity.

Marjoram too was valued for its scent. It was boiled up with rosewater and sugar to make perfumed balls to strew among clothing, and was a common constituent of herb pillows designed to promote deep sleep and fulfilling dreams. It was one of the herbs used by women keen to keep dark hair from going grey – they made an infusion mixed with sage.

Elecampane was attributed with almost magical powers. Like almost every herb worth a mention, it was held to be helpful against the plague, as well as the more prosaic but omnipresent problems like worms. An ancient physic garden herb, revered by the

LEFT: The great shaggy spikes of Canterbury bells (*Campanula*) have given shape and colour to summer gardens for centuries.

ABOVE: 15-century courtly figures in the grounds of the Chateau de Dourdan, from the *Tres Riches Heures du Duc de Berry.*

ABOVE: 15th-century illustration of the Virgin and Child with angels in a garden.

RIGHT: Bryony (*Bryonia dioica*) is a hedgerow twiner which produces poisonous shiny scarlet berries in September.

Anglo-Saxons, with ragged yellow flowers and sticky leaves, it used to be made into an ointment for aches and pains, and a drink for chest complaints.

According to a medieval handbook, *Regimen Sanitatis Salernitanum:*

Ellecompane strengthens
each inward part,
A little loosenesse is thereby provoken,
It swayeth griefe of minde,
it cheeres the heart,
Allaieth wrath, and makes a man fair
spoken:
And drunk with Rew in wine,
it doth impart
Great help to those that have
their bellies broken.

Plainly what every happy home needs, and the virtue of tranquilizing hot tempers was one which it shared with loosestrife whose common name comes from the Greek *lusimachon*, meaning 'ending strife'.

MEDICINAL HERBS

There were many other medicinal herbs of the summer months. Country people still collect agrimony with which to make a tonic tea. It has been used to treat dry coughs, lumbago,

liver complaints, rheumatism, and bladder problems, and was one of the fifty seven herbs which made up the 'Holy Salve' used by the Anglo-Saxons against poisons and evil.

Rue (*Ruta graveolens*), the 'herb of grace', was used to make a skin tonic and cleanser, and was also an aromatic strewing herb.

Fennel too had mystical properties. It was one of the nine sacred and all-powerful herbs lauded in the tenth-century Anglo-Saxon *Lacnunga* as having the power to protect

against just about every evil known, including worm blast, thistle blast, dusky venom, flying things and loathed things. Its delicate, feathery leaves have been used for all stomach and digestive problems, to improve eyesight and memory, and to cure rheumatism and cramps. It was credited with powers against all kinds of pain, with promoting general good health and prolonging life. Its seeds were chewed to allay the pangs of religious fasting and simple starvation. Sir John Harington put the ancient lore into a neat form which encapsulates the general and positive feeling about fennel:

In Fennel-seed, this vertue
you shall finde,
Foorth of your lower parts to
drive the winde.
Of Fennel vertues foure they do recite,
First, it hath power some poysons
to expell,
Next, burning Agues it will put to
flight,
The stomack it doth cleanse,
and comfort well:
And fourthly, it doth keepe
and cleanse the sight,
And thus the seede and hearbe
doth both excell.

Feverfew was another favourite, happy to thrive on neglect, impossible to mistake for anything else and producing an endless succession of pretty white flowers and finely cut aromatic leaves, feverfew was the familiar medieval painkiller par excellence. It was relied upon by women to ease childbirth and by gluttons to: 'Cleanse the kidneys and cheer the heart, when taken in wine.' It was grown commercially as well as having a much frequented corner in every cottage garden.

Comfrey, whose common names 'knitbone', 'bruisewort', 'boneset' and 'knitback' give a hint of its properties, was used to promote the healing of bruises, fractures and burns. It can heal tissue thanks to a constituent (allantoin) that can actually penetrate the skin and help connective tissue, bone and cartilage to grow. It was used as a poultice, and was also taken internally to cure stomach and digestive problems, though now there is some controversy about possible side-effects. It was also made into a skin cream to cure chapped or rough hands.

Tansy has a flavour that is just about impossible for the twentieth-century palate

A scene from the *Roman de la Rose*, showing a lover courting a lady, while fountains splash, birds sing and the ground is carpeted with flowers.

BELOW LEFT: **Toadflax (*Linaria*) with St John's Wort (*Hypericum perforatum*), meadowsweet (*Filipendula ulmerla*) and ladies bedstraw (*Galium verum*).**

BELOW RIGHT: **Sweet-smelling agrimony (*Agrimonia eupatoria*) was an ingredient of potpourri and herb pillows 'Lay it under head and sleep as if dead'. . .**

to enjoy, but to medieval man, it was a valuable vermifuge, prevented the ague, and both encouraged pregnancies and terminated them. 'Let those Women that desire children love this herb, 'tis their best Companion, their Husband excepted' according to Culpepper.

All this is as may be – astounding to anyone who has thoughtfully chewed a sprig of this paraffin-flavoured herb is that the people of the Middle Ages positively relished its repellant taste. It was apparently an essential potherb used for sweet and savoury dishes, including a sort of sweet stir-fry consisting of young tansy leaves, green corn and violets, moistened with orange and sugar. Its juice was also used to flavour omelettes.

There is no accounting for medieval tastes. They tried to find some use for just about anything that grew, believing that God had put it all here for our delectation - and were likely to toss a handful of peony seeds into any dish that needed reviving. Piers Plowman mentions them:

'Hast thou,' quoth he, 'any hot spices?'
'I have pepper and peony and a pound of garlic.

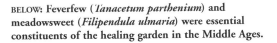

BELOW: Tansy (*Tanacetum vulgare*) bitter and sharp to our palates, was much used in cooking in the Middle Ages.

BELOW: Feverfew (*Tanacetum parthenium*) and meadowsweet (*Filipendula ulmaria*) were essential constituents of the healing garden in the Middle Ages.

A farthing worth of fennel seeds,
for fasting days I bought it.'

However, the peony seed was not solely valued for its peppery qualities. According to Gerard it had long been used as an aid to sweet sleep:

The black graines (that is the seed) to the number of fifteene taken in wine or mead is a speciall remedie for those that are troubled in the night with the disease called the Night Mare, which is as though a heavy burthen were laid upon them and they oppressed therewith, as if they were overcome with their enemies, or overprest with some great weight or burthen, and they are also good against melancholie dreames.

Not all medieval plants were beneficial. Gerard spoke feelingly for farmers in his description of corn cockle: 'What hurt it doth among corn, the spoile of bread, as well in colour, taste and unwholesomenesse, is better known than desired.'

Peonies have a fleeting but sweet fragrance, not strong enough to rate a medieval mention. Dried valerian roots, on the other

A herbal nosegay or tussie-mussie, carried to smell sweet and keep plagues and agues at bay.

hand used to be used to scent clean linen – possibly in the hope of deterring moths. The smell has noticeable effects on animals: cats and horses appear to like it, as do rodents – hence its use as bait – and malevolent dogs are calmed by it.

Meadowsweet and woodruff are both scented and fulfil similar functions, though the frothy heads of meadowsweet come into bloom later, in July. Still subject to a wide variety of poetic local names – queen of the meadow, sweet hay, courtship and matrimony, kiss-me-quick, summer's farewell – and once even known as the rather less flattering goat's beard on account of its less than odoriferous smell when fresh, dried meadowsweet was nevertheless used as a strewing herb to help mask the usual less than lovely domestic fragrances. Gerard described it later in glowing terms:

The leaves and flowers far excell all other strowing herbes, for to decke up houses, to strowe in chambers, hals, and banketting houses in the sommer time; for the smell thereof maketh the hart merrie, delighteth the senses: neither doth it cause headach, or lothsomnesse to meate, as some other sweete smelling herbes do.

It was boiled up with dandelion and agrimony, sugar, lemons and yeast to make meadowsweet beer. Its name used to be meadsweet more in reference to its use as a flavouring for mead than to its likely location.

Flavouring alcohol was obviously a concern – Queen Philippa gave a scented single pink to Henry Daniel, about which he rhapsodized: 'It is a wonder sweet and it spiceth every liquor that it be laid in, and principally red', which may be where the name 'sops in wine' started.

RIGHT: **Hollyhock (***Althaea rosea***), or 'rose of Spain', one of the most stately and dramatic of summer flowers.**

Purple loosestrife
(*Lythrum salicaria*).

LEFT: A pungent herbal bouquet, in which artemisia
(*Artemisia abrotanum*), rue (*Ruta graveolens*), St
John's Wort (*Hypericum perforatum*), lavender
(*Lavandula stoechas*), deadnettle (*Lamium
maculatum*), feverfew (*Tanacetum parthenium*),
fennel (*Foeniculum vulgare*) and borage (*Borago
officinalis*) are the dominant notes. Many of these
were essential for the unending medieval concern
with fortifying and cleansing the inner person.
There was a correct way of gathering herbs, and an
incorrect – it was important to collect them when
they were at their best and timing had to be
carefully judged. Aromatic mountain herbs were
considered to be more potent than their sappy
meadow or water-side fellows. A contemporary
writer (originally in Latin) advises further: 'The
flowers of herbs and their seeds [should be saved] in
little bags or in wooden boxes in a chest.'

Jacob's ladder
(*Polemonium*).

BELOW: Vibrant pinks and purples - corncockle
(*Agrostemma githago*), scabious (*Scabiosa*), and
borage (*Borago officinalis*).

This detail from the *Hours of the Duke of Burgundy* shows Emilia, clad in ermine and velvet, making a headdress of red and white roses threaded onto a willow framework. This tiny *hortus conclusus* is the quintessential medieval garden, walled and crenellated with neatly clipped turf seats, a scented trellis of red and white roses, a frill of gillyflowers as an edging, and an ebullient vine, trained to make a shaded tunnel. Emilia is the emblem of courtly love, and her virginal untouchability is accentuated by the two courtiers from whom she is firmly barred. The carved and ornamented arch and windows in the trellis show a low planted wall where pride of place has been given to an iris, albeit strangely barren.

Winter

Winter took some surviving. An apparently endless succession of short, cold, grey days, the air suffused with damp; rain and snow; nothing delicious to pluck from a tree or pick from the vegetable patch.

When winter walls close in, people have always had to dream up ingenious excuses to save themselves from utter despair: the Romans were never diffident about inventing a reason for a beano, and they left behind them the usual half-understood legacy of strange celebratory habits to puzzle the men of the Dark Ages. In this case, there was the week-long Saturnalia in December, and the Kalends that began in January.

CHRISTMAS

For medieval man, Christmas Day itself was a polite Christian veneer disguising the typically excessive Roman feast dedicated to the Unconquered Sun, from which the vital element of fire remains – with lights and yule logs much in evidence.

Christmas lasted the whole twelve days, beginning on Christmas Eve, and ending on Twelfth Night. The midwinter evergreens were all treated with respect and considered to be suffused with a special magic – holly (which also featured at every self-respecting

Saturnalia), yew or laurel were used to deck every possible surface, and a huge bunch of evergreens, the Christmas Bush, was hung from the ceiling.

MISTLETOE

Mistletoe was tied around a wooden frame, to make a Kissing Bush, which was further embellished with pennants of coloured cloth, nuts and fruit. Kissing has always been a popular pastime, hence the continued plunder of apple trees for their kissing cargo of mistletoe.

Gathering mistletoe was for the Druids an occasion of much ceremony and magic, with all kinds of lunar strictures, and particulars as to the host tree. Vestiges of such superstition remain to this day, and country people are still chary about when and where and how mistletoe should be gathered. It was the most important of the seven sacred Druid herbs, along with vervain, henbane, primrose, pulsatilla, clover and wolf's-bane. It was considered to be aphrodisiac, and to make women fertile. But the whole mistletoe business is deeply mysterious, and the Druidic

PREVIOUS PAGE: **Holly (*Ilex aquifolium*), ivy (*Hedera helix*) and mistletoe (*Viscum album*).**

RIGHT: **The strange and subtle colours of hellebore (*Helleborus*), which flowers between autumn and winter, and lasts for ages.**

associations may have been perverted by a later desire for a folksy frisson, and fact and fancy are now inseparable.

HOLLY

Like most plants with magic properties, holly had to be approached with caution – it could be a friend, or it could cause disaster. The wood was used to keep unfriendly spirits away, to ward off ailments afflicting children and animals, and within the confines of Christian religion, it perfectly symbolized the passion and crucifixion of Christ – milk-white flowers, blood-red berries, prickles as sharp as thorns, bark bitter as gall. People have always been superstitious about holly, considering it bad luck to burn it, chop it down, cut off branches (as distinguished from pulling them off) or in some cases to bring it indoors at all, especially at a time other than Christmas. This did not stop hungry country dwellers experimenting with it, and discovering that you could make an effective bird-lime with the juice of the bark mixed with oil. In the battle for mastery between holly and ivy, holly always wins, since it was considered to be the masculine plant, ivy the feminine. The following lines

LEFT: Holly (*Ilex aquifolium*).

RIGHT: Ivy (*Hedera helix*).

attributed to Henry VIII express this perennial struggle within nature:

> A! the holy grouth grene
> With ive all alone
> When flowerys can not be sene,
> And grene wode levys be gone.
> Grene growith the holy, so doth the ive;
> Thow wynter blastys blow never so hye,
> Grene growth the holy.

IVY

Ivy is another magic plant, with potential for good or ill – it was one of the herbs of St John and any plant that flowers in late autumn was considered to have strange powers. Like holly, it was always thought very unlucky to bring it indoors at any time other than the precise duration of Christmas, and it had to be outside again no later than January 6th. It had more prosaic uses – in laundry, as a cure for corns and burns, swollen glands and dropsy, and as a protector of livestock. It was prescribed as a soothing balm for a familiar twentieth-century complaint as far back as the Anglo-Saxon *Leech Book of Bald* (which dates from around 900 and was penned on vellum for its unfortunately named owner by a scribe called Cild): 'For sunburn boil in butter tender ivy twigs, smear therewith.'

WASSAILING

There were cheerier winter festivities. Wassailing, apart from being a transparent excuse to down a barrel of cider, was intended to make the dormant apple trees fruitful, drive away malevolent spirits and awaken the urge for growth and health. The procedure consisted of lighting fires, hitting the trees with sticks, making a deal of noise by howling or blowing a cow's horn, dancing around the most abundant tree, and generally drinking a health to the guardians of the trees on the eve of Christmas and Epiphany, or the eve of the old Twelfth Night, January 17th:

Old apple tree, old apple tree,
We've come to wassail thee,
To bear and to bow apples enow,
Hats full, caps full, three bushel bags full,
Barn floors full and a little heap under the stairs.

It was particularly auspicious if the sun shone on the trees at the nadir of the year:

If wold Christmas Day be fair and bright
Ye'd have apples to your heart's delight.

Mistletoe (*Viscum album*), believed to have magical powers.

After wassailing the next heart-lifting event before spring proper is Valentine's Day – in medieval times this was all about aphrodisiac carryings-on, inflamed perhaps by special music, food, drink, and bowls of fragrant herbs – rosemary, yarrow, marjoram. Herbs were also burned in candles and on fires, and the air was scented with bay and resinous pine. Herbs found their way into Valentine salads, whether to calm or impassion is hard to say. And if all else failed, medieval maidens could resort to divination by hemp-seed (similar to reading tea-leaves), yarrow leaves or eringoes (yarrow, rosemary and sea holly placed on or in the pillow to cause prophetic dreams, or, more likely, rather painfully scratched faces).

The Christmas rose (*Helleborus niger*) is another plant with a dubious reputation – it dates back to Neolithic times, and was grown outside cottage doors to protect the inhabitants from evil. It was used, and abused, medicinally – considered an effective purgative and vermifuge, it had the unfortunate side-effect of occasionally killing the sufferer. Its strange, unseasonal flowers put one in mind of the sinister and morbid, but anything that flowers in midwinter is to be welcomed, and medieval cottagers were quite happy to give it a shady corner in which to spread its jagged leaves and modestly downcast blooms.

By contrast, quinces were unequivocally valued for their sour, hard fruit, which was treated with lavish doses of almond milk, egg yolks, spices and saffron to make sweet jellies, pastries and pies. A medieval recipe for quince marmalade is so smothered with sweet and alcoholic extras that you could probably substitute mangel-wurzels for the quinces and end up with something delicious.

Peel and quarter the quinces, taking out the pips, and the eye at the end. Boil them in a good red wine and run them through a strainer. Boil a large amount of honey a long time. Skim it and set the quinces in it. Stir well and bring to the boil until the honey is reduced by half. Add hippocras. Stir until cold, and cut into pieces to serve.

Hippocras was a wine flavoured with spices. Winter was not all misery.

Medieval gardens to visit

One of the miracles of medieval gardens is that they still exist – albeit in skilful recreations. With a shred of imagination you can transport yourself across the centuries and muse upon eternal verities and the innocent symbolism of rose and violet, iris and daisy. Another miracle is that their neat compactness makes them infinitely adaptable – you can fit a medieval corner into a tiny wedge of ground between tall buildings, or tack it onto the fringes of a romantic country garden, and there are cleverly researched and planted examples to show you what the planting can look like, and how to take the best from historic inspiration and marry it with a breezier and more casual contemporary modus vivendi.

For true medievalists there are gardens to suit every whim – whether you have a penchant to see herbers,

RIGHT: **The gardens of Prieure Notre Dame d'Orsan, showing the wooden arbours which were such a feature of medieval gardens.**

BELOW: **A leafy tunnel at Orsan.**

arbours, lady gardens, or architectural features in the pentice and tunnel mode, the former a particular kind of slope-roofed shelter favoured by medieval garden designers. And nothing beats having a good look in person – you can never get the feeling of a garden through verbal description and pictures alone. There are no words that can do justice to the utter serendipity of sitting surrounded by the simple scented flowers that have an atavistic half-remembered folk-history of legend. So, these are the gardens to visit.

QUEEN ELEANOR'S GARDEN

If you happen to be in Great Britain, the perfect pocket-handkerchief is to be found in the grounds of Winchester Castle. Here is an exquisite thirteenth-century triangle, Queen Eleanor's garden, mostly lapped by ancient walls, and reconstructed from descriptions of seven or eight royal gardens of the time. The materials used for the architecture – the channel and fountain, the benches and pentice – have an integrity which is in keeping with the period, the Great Hall and its contents. Lead, bronze, Purbeck limestone ashlar blend seamlessly with the crumbling sense of antiquity surrounding them. The

TOP, ABOVE, AND RIGHT: **Various views of the Priory at Orsan, showing raised beds enclosed with wattle fencing in the medieval style.**

plants are all apposite too, with the essential mixture of medicinal, laundry, edible and decorative herbs and flowers making a fragrant pot-pourri, with a camomile carpet beneath your feet and a turf seat upon which to sit. Queen Eleanor herself is credited with introducing the rose of Spain, known more

prosaically these days as the hollyhock, whose tall pink spires quiver high above narrow beds of poppies, marigolds, lilies, mallow, aquilegia and campanula. The turf is speckled with speedwell, wild strawberry, violets and hawkweed. Holly, broom, hawthorn, ivy and bay all grow laden with impeccable Christian symbolism, and even the ineradicable weeds – such as the mare's tail and butcher's broom which, once rooted, grow invincibly for ever – had a use as early protoypes for scrubbing brushes and scouring pads. This is a tiny contemplative garden par excellence, and shows brilliantly what can be achieved with simple plants in a confined space.

ABOVE: *Macrocephala.*

RIGHT: **The contemplative garden of the Abbaye Royale at Fontevraud.**

BELOW: **Illustration from Pliny's *Historia Naturalis.***

WEALD & DOWNLAND MUSEUM

Sylvia Landsberg, the designer of Queen Eleanor's Garden has been responsible for a handful more in the South of England, all well worth visiting: Bayleaf and Hangleton at the Weald and Downland Museum are two, which recreate the kind of gardens that might have belonged to less illustrious fifteenth- and thirteenth-century villagers respectively. Here in the open air Museum you will find all the vegetables, fruit, herbers and arbours, wattle fencing and livestock (in the form of bees and a pig) that were deemed essential for life, though the two gardens span the extremes of prosperity and subsistence. This is a fascinating historical exercise, brilliantly achieved, but with fewer ideas that a twentieth-century gardener might wish to replicate in their own garden.

ABOVE: *Dianthus caryophyllus* and wild strawberry (*Fragaria vesca*).

LEFT: The 15th-century garden of Sir Roger Vaughan at Tretower Court, Powys, showing the pergola twined with roses and vines and the weathered fencing enclosing the fountain.

SHREWSBURY

Brother Cadfael's Garden in Shrewsbury, on the other hand, is full of decorative features that could bring a calming and contemplative air to the most sophisticated contemporary garden. This twelfth century physic garden, also the work of Sylvia Landsberg, is packed with small and charming corners evoking the serious pleasures of the monastic life. Here is a retreat in which the fictitious herbalist might have pursued his studies and an arbour in which he might have sat, surrounded by vines and poisonous bryony – a fitting memento mori for the medically minded – to write his notes. The layout was based on the surviving plan for the Christ Church herbarium at Canterbury, which fortuitously happened to occupy a very similar plot of land, roughly 50 feet by 30. The carefully appropriate planting has been made using the works of Aelfric, Macer, Neckam and the Myddfai for absolute authenticity.

TRETOWER COURT

Sir Roger Vaughan's fifteenth-century garden at Tretower Court in Powys is rather grander, as befits a courtier's retreat. It is surrounded by apple trees, beneath which you can sit and admire the mammoth rose and vine-thatched pergola, 40 yards long, beneath which is a speckled carpet of woodruff and aquilegia, cornflower and Lily of the valley. Weathered fencing contains a chequerboard of turf and flowers centred with a fountain, and the whole adds up to a timeless rural idyll, set in the peaceful Usk Valley, in which to dream of knights and chivalric business. Midsummer is

LEFT AND ABOVE: The simple medieval gardens at the Weald and Downland Museum, recreated by Sylvia Landsberg.

the moment to experience the cascading roses at their fragrant best.

ORSAN

For mobile medievalists there are three interesting medieval gardens which have been lovingly recreated in France. Most spectacularly, Les Jardins du Prieuré Notre Dame d'Orsan south of Blois, have just about everything that any self-respecting slice of history should have, and the garden has been designed to look good from the foliage and blossom of May until the fruit ripens in October. The summer is heady with roses, lavender, a rainbow of flowers and a beautifully laid out vegetable garden. There are rustic wooden arbours that make you just want to rush home and get busy with a bit of simple carpentry. This garden was created almost as an afterthought by the extremely talented and dedicated architects who fell in love with the Priory itself. Having completed the major and necessary repairs to the building, they turned to its surroundings. Their architectural penchant resulted in a sculptural collection of airy outdoor follies, each of which is more seductive than the last – this is a beautifully assembled interpretation of the spirit of the medieval jardin clos, where basic materials have been used with ingenuity and inspiring elegance.

POITOU

Le Jardin Carolingian at Poitou is the product of scrupulous research and is a plant historian's interestingly documented Mecca. This is Charlemagne's list of essential plants made manifest in the garden attached to the ancient royal silver mines at Melle. These are the plants necessary for life – the roots,

cereals, medicinal and flavouring herbs that fed and healed.

FONTEVRAUD

The Abbaye Royale of Fontevraud has a contemplative and cloistered garden, that strongly evokes the kind of quiet rumination pursued by medieval nuns and monks. The setting, near Chinon, is quite beautiful, and the buildings are in effect a monastic city composed of four priories: 'Le Grand Moutier' for nuns, 'La Madeleine' for lay sisters who tended the gardens and did the work; 'Saint-Lazare' and 'Saint-Benoit' for the nursing sisters, and 'Saint-Jean-de-l'Habit' for all the monks and priests.

BEBENHAUSEN ABBEY

Courtyards and cloisters are part of the architectural richness of Bebenhausen Abbey near Tubingen, just south of Stuttgart, also. These have at their heart another small and unpretentious medieval garden, in which to calm the troubled heart and contemplate the extraordinary architectural achievements of man in the centuries before print. This is a simple garden which is best appreciated if vistied en passant, but it is nonetheless evocative in its own way. Nothing beats sitting surrounded by the plants from which our garden familiars were bred, and quietly drinking in the serene legacy of one thousand years of religious devotion.

LEFT: **The peaceful contemplative garden of Bebenhausen Abbey, south of Stuttgart.**

BELOW: **The Carolingien Gardens at Melle in France.**

Medieval garden design

Information about medieval garden design comes from the illuminated manuscripts and Books of Hours of the extremely wealthy, and the plans of monasteries. The literature of the time does not summon up images that can be used by the interested reader to plan their own garden, though the pleasures of a private place filled with flowers, scents, birds and water are described with innocent conviction and poetic enthusiasm, from Walafrid Strabo's 9th century 'Hortulus' (Little Garden) onwards.

The surviving ninth-century plan of the Benedictine Monastery of St Gall in Switzerland provides a model, the epitome of logic, economy and good sense from which there was little need to deviate. The monastery garden was divided into three: a physic garden or herbarium from which the infirmarers gathered their medicinal herbs – it was the monks who kept the herbal tradition alive; a kitchen garden neatly laid out with narrow strips of carrots, onions, beets, salad and culinary herbs; and a cemetery with neatly trained fruit and nut trees which could do service as a pomerium.

Flowers were of little importance in themselves, apart from providing a colourful, scented, soothing and meditation-inducing subtext of religious imagery - we should all be grateful to the Virgin Mary for making the lush sensuous hedonism of roses and lilies perfectly acceptable, in fact essential, in the 'Mary' gardens created in her honour.

Clairvaux was described thus: 'Behind the abbey but within the wall of the cloister, there is a wide level ground; here there is an orchard, with a great many different fruit trees, quite like a small wood. It is close to the infirmary and is very conforting to the brothers, providing a wide promenade for those who want to walk, and a pleasant resting place for those who prefer to rest. Where the orchard leaves off, the garden begins, divided into several beds or cut up by little canals, which though of standing water, do flow more or less. The water fulfills the double purpose of nourishing the fish and watering the vegetables.' Some orders of monks had their own private gardens for meditation alongside their cells.

RIGHT:
Vine Arbour, Villandoy, France.

FAR RIGHT:
Vine Arbour, Queen Eleanor's Garden, England.

HORTUS CONCLUSUS

As life became less embattled, pleasure gardens began to be cultivated by the nobility. At first they tended to be the Hortus Conclusus – a confined walled garden, which tended to be within the safe precincts of the moat – which demanded architectural formality to suit its surroundings. This blended into the notion of a garden within a garden, taking the mysterious and provocative Song of Solomon as inspiration: 'A garden enclosed is my sister, my spouse; a spring shut up, a fountain sealed. Thy plants are an orchard of pomegranates, with pleasant fruits: spikenard and saffron, calamus and cinnamon, with all trees of frankincense; myrrh and aloes, with all the chief spices.'

Gradually, as confidence increased, larger and less geometric gardens away from the castle walls were enjoyed, known as the viridarium, with trees, water tanks and channels, shady walks and arbours.

As courtly love superseded religious devotion, gardens evolved into the Hortus Deliciarum, which trod a delicate line between chivalry and cupidity. In fact the gardens did not change as much as the human activities within them, and sensuous pleasures took over from sober prayer and rosary beads, as documented in the *Roman de la Rose* and by Chaucer and Boccaccio. Albertus Magnus describes such a garden evocatively: 'There are . . . what are called pleasure gardens. There may be planted every sweet-smelling herb such as rue, and sage and basil, and likewise all sorts of flowers, as the violet, columbine, lily, rose, iris and the like. So that between these herbs and the turf, at the edge of the lawn set square, let there be a higher bench of turf flowering and lovely; and somewhere in the middle provide seats so that men may sit down there to take their repose pleasurably when their senses need refreshment. Upon the lawn, too, against the heat of the sun, trees should be planted or vines trained, so that the lawn may have a delightful and cooling shade, sheltered by their leaves. . . . Care should also

TOP TO BOTTOM: **From the garden at Orsan, a woven seat of wattle around a tree; a simple curved seat under a leafy canopy; a wattle arbour with raised staging for showing off various plants in pots.**

be taken that the trees are not too close together or too numerous, for cutting off the breeze may do harm to health. . . . Let them be sweet trees, with perfumed flowers and agreeable shade, like grape-vines, pears, pomegranates, sweet bay trees, cypresses and such like.'

PUBLIC GARDENS

Charlemagne, who took an informed and benign interest in horticulture and gardens, began a tradition for public gardens or managed parks in which people could stroll in a paradise complete with peacocks and swans, wooded glades and archery tunnels. These were called Pratum in Latin, and gave that name to important gardens in Madrid, Vienna and Paris. The occasional maze is mentioned, though not illustrated. There are plenty of ideas in medieval gardens that would contribute a tranquilizing charm to the way we live today. Most of the documentary evidence comes from the illuminated manuscripts commissioned by wealthy nobility, so they are not widely representative. But the middle classes could adapt most of the elements – as we can today.

The wealthy had space, they had teams of workmen and gardeners, and they could acquire grand accessories of the bronze fountain, hexagonal marble table and carved stone bench variety. These expensive items aside, medieval gardening requires nothing beyond the most basic bricklaying, woodwork and gardening skills.

HERBERS

The idea of the garden as an outdoor room is one to which we pay lip service today, but do not take nearly as far as they did in the Middle Ages. Their herbers were more literally rooms in that they were small, seriously walled or fenced about. There was a wide variety of fencing materials and styles, ranging from beautifully laid growing hedge plants to wooden trellis or hazel wattle intertwined with willow wands, rails, chestnut palisades or oak pickets. These were generally covered with vines or climbing red and white roses, and sometimes had elaborate windows and doors cut in them. Outer fences were often freshly cut poles, interwoven with withies in the manner of a skilfully laid hedge. Since these poles must have rooted as often as not, the

two were probably indistinguishable. It was all too easy for outsiders to bend the poles and get in, so the gardens had good solid outer walls, with locked gates.

An elaborate design in wattle fencing at Orsan, ready to provide seating against a background of twining roses.

TURF BENCHES

Very likely there would be a turf bench around three of the walls, either built up on bricks, held in place with wattle, on a wooden framework, or simply grassed top and sides –

not in fact simple at all, and apt to crumble away at the first shower of rain. This might also have herbs such as thyme or camomile planted among the grass to release a waft of sharp perfume when bruised.

FLOWERS

At the back of the turf seat irises, rocket, aquilegia, peonies and carnations were often planted against the wall. Or there might be a free-standing raised seat, a hybrid between raised flower beds and turf benches, enclosing an area of grass or flower beds well within the walls of the garden surrounded by a path. There were herbaceous borders against the walls in some gardens – a narrow ribbon of flowers, just one plant deep.

The central space between the walls and the seats was usually simply grass, clipped as close as a carpet. This could be further embellished and take the form of a flowery mead pied with tiny flowers – daisies, pimpernel and speedwell. Other additions familiar from tapestries and paintings are aquilegia, bistort,

camomile, campion, carnations, dandelions, forget-me-not, irises, lilies and Lily of the valley, Lords and Ladies, orchids, periwinkle, stock, strawberries, sweet rocket, violas. This was eventually considered old-fashioned, and was superseded by lawns of plain jewel-green grass – possibly the admixture of flowers made upkeep of the gardens too problematical, and control of nature became the dominant obsession.

PATHS

Further complexity and structure is added if the grassed area is broken up by paths. Formal sand, gravel or chessboard paving paths were edged with rails, along which were grown low red and white double roses (*Rosa gallica* and *Rosa alba*) or stickadove lavender. These would enclose chequer formation beds filled with small plants plus a specimen bush or standard tree. In some manuscripts, the squares and rectangles of bedding appear to be laid out like bejewelled rugs: flat areas of grass intersected by paths and sprinkled with tiny bright flowers.

Alternatively flower beds were slightly raised on wood, stone or brick edges, and

ABOVE: **The raised beds at Orsan.**

ABOVE: **The herb garden at Orsan, enclosed with wattle fencing.**

LEFT: **Close-up of the raised marrow beds again enclosed with wattle.**

occasionally railed as well. Sometimes they were made more ornate still – with a pyramid of three tiers or seats, known as an estrade, stacked up like a wedding cake and held wattle collars, as a setting for a specimen tree.

TREES

Trees were subjected to an ingenious range of treatments. Like living sculpture, they were grafted, espaliered, pleached, pruned and pollarded. They were shaped into tall triple-tiered cake-stands or, in the case of fruit trees, open goblet shapes in order to facilitate ripening, or trained on flexible four-spoked, wheel-shaped frameworks made of willow. Small evergreens like box were clipped into bobbles on stems and planted in the centre of a quincunx of small specimen shrubs. The ingenuity of medieval gardeners did not stop with clipping the canopy – saplings were shaped around poles to end up with sophisticated corkscrew shapes and dramatic spirals topped by a froth of greenery.

FRUIT TREES

Medieval gardeners were particularly fond of fruiting trees since they have everything one could possibly wish for: fragrant blossom in spring, a feathery canopy of leaves during hot summer afternoons, and fruit come the autumn. This made orchards vulnerable, and serious fruit growers were known to construct a moat around their wattle fenced trees, in order to keep the scrumpers at bay. The trees appear to have been routinely and rigorously pruned because they have a mop-headed neatness uncharacteristic of fruit trees allowed to go their own way. Apples, pears and cherries were common, augmented with more exotic fruit and nuts such as chestnuts, medlars, quinces, walnuts and mulberries.

ARBOURS

Arbours and airy open pergolas, tunnels and cloistered walkways on wooden frameworks were all smothered with vines or roses. The tunnels had shaped domes at the intersections of one path with another, ensuring shade and total privacy for the length of the walk. Trelliswork was made of straight poles tied at the diagonal intersections with twine. Trellis was also laid horizontally as a framework for carnations and floppy flowers. Medieval gardeners also made wooden tripods and cane 'staples' for the same purpose. Pleaching was a skill which they would use to make airy pavilions and arbours.

ROOF–TOP GARDENS

Roof-top gardens on the beetling pinnacles of castles, and balconies were carefully nurtured with estrade trees in pots, pergolas, and vine canopies. Wind and water must have been the problems, they still are today in this kind of exposed situation. The reward must have been stupendous with breathtaking panoramic views framed by fragrant rose-covered trellis and teetering pots of pinks.

The myriad possibilities of pots, vases, window-boxes were all exploited by medieval gardeners, who used them much as people do

The fountain surrounded by turf and flowers in Sir Roger Vaughan's garden in Powys.

today, to make a fugitive splash of colour or point of interest which could be replaced when the flowering was over. Large pots were placed under trees filled with pinks grown on wicker frameworks which slotted into holes in the rim, and window-boxes of wood were filled with small jewel-like flowers and cantilevered somewhat perilously outside castle windows. Permanent and expensive garden features are plentifully illustrated in Books of Hours and manuscripts.

GREAT GARDENS

Really grand gardens contained gothic gloriettes of wood or stone, some serious brick and stone buildings with open colonnaded fronts or loggias, and most were equipped with all the necessary paraphernalia for comfortable eating and drinking. There were banqueting pavilions, canopied seats with tapestry or brocade hung from poles, and stone and wood benches set about permanent octagonal tables, a perch made less chilly by sumptuous tasselled cushions. Recessed seats were built of stone, wood or brick and were planted with the usual fragrant floral and herbal cushions. Simple wooden octagonal summer-houses with tiled floors and unglazed windows overlooked the formal gardens. An appealing view from windows was always important, and the usual formal garden layout was crammed with as much colour and incident as possible.

WATER

Grand gardens also made copious use of water. Springs, streams and rills might meander through the backyards of the poor, but moats and fountains of stone or metal were the prerogative of the rich. There were simple water-tanks such as every Islamic garden aspires to, but with just one stream leading out of the garden (as opposed to the four rivers of life), with fish, and big dipping spoons chained to the edge to provide drinking water for over-heated revellers. There were also complex and fanciful fountains of carved stone – like the fonts in medieval churches – or of strangely wrought metal, topped by heraldic beasts. The cooling, soothing sound of water was much prized.

ENJOYING GARDEN LIFE

Within this paradise, those with time on their hands could indulge in a range of activities – chess, swimming in moats, eating and drinking, dancing to the music of harp, oboe, fife-and-drum, reading or dashing off the odd love poem, playing with babies, practising music, gossiping, the ubiquitous and perennial garland and posy making, spinning and weaving. There were also public gardens for archery and bowls. To animate the scene there were pets and diverse

The fountain at Prieure d'Orsan.

creatures encouraged to wander – peacocks and swans lent an air of elegance – and there were song-birds – flying free and in cages.

The medieval garden was a true paradise, in short, and a happy retreat from an uncertain world outside. Nothing much has changed and we might all enjoy the benefits of such a refuge today.

Medieval plant directory

The plants featured in this directory have been arranged broadly into their natural flowering order and will provide a reliable starting point in the recreation of any medieval garden today.

DAFFODIL
(Narcissus)

Spring-flowering bulb. Happy growing in grass, in sun or partial shade, where they come up obligingly year after year in ever-increasing clumps. Allow the leaves to yellow before cutting them down. Plant in holes three times deeper than the bulb, in well-fertilized soil, which ideally should be well-drained without drying out.

PRIMROSE
(Primula vulgaris)

Grow from seed in partial shade, and do not allow the seedlings to dry out. Plant 9 in (20 cm) apart. The primrose produces trusses of pale sulphur yellow flowers in March and April. They like fertile soil: well-decayed manure or organic fertilizer is abundantly rewarded, and they need to keep moist.

COWSLIP
(Primula veris)

Growing conditions as for primrose. The seed should be sown in autumn in situ, or in trays in a cold frame. Happy in sun or partial shade, cowslips were once common, growing on grassy roadside banks, though they have become much more rare due to over-picking and spraying. They can be increased by root division.

VIOLET
(Viola odorata)

A perennial which produces fragrant purple and white flowers 4–6 in (10–15 cm) tall from February to April. Grow from seed in autumn in moist, rich, shady or semi-shaded soil. Once established, violets will self-seed and spread by runners wherever they have a mind to.

WHITE DEADNETTLE
(Lamium maculatum)

An invasive and somewhat coarse ground-cover plant. Best suited to the wild garden and ordinary garden soil, the deadnettle can be grown very easily from root cuttings in autumn. The plant is happy whether in sun or shade, and the spikes should be sheared off after flowering to encourage the handsome marbled foliage.

LORDS AND LADIES
(Arum maculatum)

One of the most common wild flowers. Its fragrance of decomposing manure attracts pollinating flies – very successfully, judging by its omnipresence and the number of sinister glossy red poisonous berries it produces in July and August. The 9–18 in (23–45 cm) white spathes unfurl in April.

RAMSONS
(Allium ursinum)

BUGLE
(Ajuga reptans)

HERB ROBERT
(Geranium robertianum)

Otherwise known as wild garlic. Happy in shaded, damp woodland soil, ramsons grow wild in large clumps, which can be divided in the autumn and transplanted, if you want to inhale the odd whiff of garlic as you wander your garden in April to June. The shiny white star flowers are 6–15 in (15–37 cm) tall, and the plant is credited with healing powers: 'Eat leckes in lide (March) and ramsins in May/And all the year after physitians may play.'

Whorls of steely blue flowers which grow in May and June from green or bronzed foliage make excellent ground cover in moist, shady positions. The plants grow easily from divisions, too easily for some, since it also spreads rapidly by runners and can become an invasive pest.

The most common geranium, herb robert grows up to 18 in (45 cm) tall and adapts itself to a wide variety of habitats, including damp woodland, hedge banks, and seashore shingle. It has delicate, fernlike leaves with a red tinge, and produces small five-petalled pink flowers all summer long.

HONESTY
(Lunaria annua)

PERIWINKLE
(Vinca minor)

BLUEBELL
(Hyacinthoides non-scripta)

A slightly ragged-looking tall mauve or white biennial with decorative seed-heads which self-seeds generously wherever it is happy – ideally in light soil and partial shade. Sow seed in May or June, and plant out 6 in (15 cm) apart in September. The Latin name comes from the papery white circular seed-casing which is reminiscent of a tiny moon. It grows wild in waste land.

An evergreen ground-cover shrub, somewhat invasive and apt to layer itself inextricably among other plants. Plant in shady soil under trees, where it performs well, providing wands of glossy green leaves and sparse, sky-blue flowers from March until Midsummer, with occasional flowers until autumn. It will grow very easily from stem sections and layers planted straight in the soil in September, March or April, or from cuttings taken in March.

The 12 in (30 cm) tall spires of familiar sky-blue flowers, making azure carpets in open woodland, are a sign that spring has arrived. Bluebells grow from bulbs in sun or partial shade, and will occasionally throw up a white or pink sport. They should be planted 4–6 in (10–15 cm) deep from bulbs and offsets which will speedily clump up and spread. The seeds too will ripen and broadcast themselves around the parent plant – they take two or three years to flower. They like moist soil and plenty of humus.

FORGET-ME-NOT
(Myosotis)

A hardy biennial which self-sows, producing sprays of slightly fragrant bright blue flowers from May to June. They are equally happy in sun or shade, but thrive in well-drained soil with plenty of organic matter, in partial shade. Grow from seed outside in April or May, and plant out in September.

SOLOMON'S SEAL
(Polygonatum multiflorum)

A very tough herbaceous perennial, 2–4 ft (60–120 cm) tall, with arching leaf-sprays and pendulous white flowers. It grows well in shade and enjoys peaty soil and leaf-mould under trees and shrubs. Propagate from root divisions in October and March, and ensure that the plant does not dry out. Cut the mature plants down in November. Solomon's Seal can be sown from seed, but patience is essential, as the seeds may take over a year to germinate.

SPURGE
(Euphorbia)

One of a huge genus of 2000 species, most of which are toxic to humans, and which exude a characteristic irritant milky sap. The green flowers grow in separate clusters of male and female, and they are produced all summer long. Sun spurge (*Euphorbia helioscopia*) is a common weed which is found in wasteland and arable land.

CRAB-APPLE
(Malus sylvestris)

Hardy deciduous trees with decorative, self-pollinating, slightly scented flowers. The small hard fruit is traditionally made into jellies and preserves. They make neat well-shaped trees when grown as standards, and the flowers range from white, through pink to magenta, depending on the variety. They are happy in well-drained soil, with generous doses of well-rotted manure or compost. Once the shape is established they do not need pruning.

WALLFLOWER
(Cheiranthus cheiri)

Hardy sub-shrubby perennials which deteriorate after the first year and for this reason are usually grown annually from seed sown in May or June and planted out in October. They thrive in sunshine and ordinary garden soil, treated with lime if it is acid. Pinch out the tips of the plants when they are 6 in (15 cm) tall to make them bushy.

HAWTHORN
(Crataegus monogyna)

Rounded trees which grow to 30 ft (10 m) tall and whose berries and flowers are used to treat heart complaints and blood pressure problems, having the extraordinary ability to normalize both low and high blood pressure. A feature of traditional mixed hedges, heavily scented white blossom smothers the trees in May (hence the common name). They are hardy to most extremes of weather, and thrive in sunny positions in ordinary soil.

CAMPION
(Silene dioica)

COW PARSLEY
(Anthriscus sylvestris)

LUNGWORT
(Pulmonaria officinalis)

Red and white campion are leggy hedgerow plants, producing red or white flowers with an inflated calyx behind the five indented petals. They are found until midsummer in the wild in shady woodland and arable land respectively.

A charming and ubiquitous weed that belongs to a large family of similar-looking plants, some of which are most poisonous – hemlock and cowbane for example. Cow parsley adapts happily to life in all kinds of different habitats: hedgerows, woodland, roadside verges, and in spring it foams with white umbelliferous flowers in airy abundance.

Spotted leaves, and croziers of flowers in April and May that mature from pink to blue as they open, characterize this shade-loving herbaceous perennial. Seeds can be sown out of doors in April, or the plant can be increased more speedily by division in October or March. They do not like to dry out, and appreciate mulching in summer.

COLUMBINE
(Aquilegia vulgaris)

BUTTERCUP
(Ranunculus)

GUELDER ROSE
(Viburnum opulus)

A cottage garden essential, with short-spurred pink, blue or white flowers on an elegant leggy plant with ferny glaucous foliage in May and June. Sow ripe seeds in July or August, and plant out into ordinary garden soil the following September. They are equally happy in sun or partial shade, and enjoy a moist, well-drained, leafy soil. Cut the plants down after flowering.

Familiar glossy golden flowers from June to August and leggy growth in a hardy perennial which is usually an ineradicable garden pest. However, if you do introduce buttercups to your garden, they will respond well to ordinary soil, sun or partial shade, and can be increased by division of the parent plant.

A deciduous shrub that can grow to a rounded bushy plant up to 15 ft (5 m) tall, covered in May and June with great white snowballs of heavily scented flowers, which in autumn become poisonous translucent red berries. They grow readily from cuttings taken in late summer, and should be planted out, when they have reached a suitable size possibly 2–3 years later in September to March.

GARDEN POPPY
(Papaver rhoeas)

OPIUM POPPY
(Papaver somniferum)

FIELD POPPY
(Papaver rhoeas)

The garden poppy cultivated from the wild field poppy, is a delicate, ethereal flower with silky, overlapping petals in reds, pinks and white and pale green lobed leaves. The flowers – familiar scarlet in the wild – nod on their slender stems from June to August. Sow seed in situ in March in a sunny position and well-drained soil.

The opium poppy ranges in colour from a somewhat muddy and unsatisfactory mauve, to vibrant pinks, purples and scarlets. The flowers are followed by handsome seed-cases, which look good when dried. It is an annual and grows 2–3 ft (30–60 cm) tall with smooth glaucous foliage. It flowers from June to August. Best grown in a well-drained sunny position, using seeds sown in situ in March, April or September.

Poppies are a genus of 100 species of annuals, biennial and perennials. They are mostly characterized by their graceful stems, silky, tissue-fine petals in reds, pinks and whites and shaggy, deeply-cut foliage.

WILD STRAWBERRY
(Fragaria vesca)

THYME
(Thymus vulgaris)

CHIVES
(Allium schoenoprasum)

The wild strawberry grows in open woodland and hedgerows, particularly in limy soils, and produces pretty white five-petalled flowers from April until July, followed by tiny delicious red berries.

A hardy evergreen, which grows 4–6 in (10–15 cm) tall, and in June is covered with mauve flowers which bees adore. It thrives in full sun, in a gritty, well-drained soil. Divide plants in March or April, or take cuttings in May or June to plant out in early autumn.

A hardy perennial herb that speedily makes grassy green clumps of tubular leaves topped by decorative edible pinky mauve pompom flowers in June and July. They are happy in sun or semi-shade, and do not like to dry out. Grow from seeds planted in March and plant out in May, or divide existing plants in September or October.

ROSEMARY
(Rosmarinus officinalis)

MONK'S-HOOD
(Aconitum napellus)

FRENCH LAVENDER
(Lavandula stoechas)

An evergreen aromatic shrub, covered with milky blue flowers in March and April. It can grow to 7 ft (2 m) in height, and spread 6 ft (1.75 m) in width, but if it threatens to take over your garden, it is quite happy to be cut back to the desired size and shape in April. It grows very easily from cuttings taken in September or March and planted where they are to grow. It likes good drainage and sun.

All parts of this plant are poisonous to people and animals. Monk's-hood is a hardy herbaceous perennial, growing 3 ft (1 m) tall, with deeply cut leaves. Spikes of dark blue flowers are a valuable addition to borders, and flower in July and August. It grows happily in moist deep soil, and partial shade, and appreciates a summer mulch. Propagate by root division between October and March, or sow seeds in March or April and plant out in October. Cut back the spikes after flowering.

An evergreen shrub, whose grey foliage and curious fragrant purple flowers with their insect-like bracts make it a valuable addition to garden schemes, both formal and romantic. It grows 24 in (60 cm) high and wide, and is easy to propagate from cuttings taken in August and planted out the following March. The plants should be trimmed in late summer, and again in April to encourage bushiness.

DYER'S GREENWEED
(Genista tinctoria)

TURKSCAP LILY
(Lillium pyrenaicum)

FOXGLOVE
(Digitalis purpurea)

Otherwise known as woad-waxen, its dye is concentrated in the flowers which are best used fresh. It is a plant of rough pasture and roadside verge which is very happy on clay soils. It flowers in July and August and may reach 6 ft (2 m) in height. Grow from seed which should be filed before sowing to assist germination.

The yellow turkscap lily flowers in late spring and produces a tall 4 ft (1.35 m) spike of up to 12 blooms with characteristic recurved petals and an unfortunate smell. Propagate with bulb scales in summer, and grow in a sunny, well-drained spot.

A hardy perennial, which naturalizes freely in woodland. The plants tend to deteriorate, so perfectionists may wish to grow them as biennials. The pink, purple or white flower spikes grow from a rosette of rich green leaves, last from June to July and grow up to 5 ft (1.5 m) tall. Sow the tiny seeds out of doors in May or June, and plant out in partial shade in September. They do not like to dry out in summer.

PEONY
(Paeonia mascula)

PEONY
(Paeonia officinalis)

IRIS
(Iris 'orris')

Herbaceous perennials 3 ft (1 m) tall producing silky single pink, purple, or white flowers in May and June, with prominent tufts of bright yellow anthers and glossy green foliage. The flowers are followed by boat-shaped seed-cases filled with black seeds. Once established they are very long-lived, but they may take years to flower, and do not like root-disturbance. Sow seeds in September, and plant out into a nursery bed the following May. When they are large enough to fend for themselves, plant out into their flowering positions in autumn or spring. Or you can divide and replant established peonies in September. They like well-composted moist soil, in sun or semi-shade.

The clump-forming single red 'apothecaries' peony with large satiny flowers in May and June. It grows from tubers which can be split and grown as for Paeonia mascula. There are many double forms which have superseded the true species, and which flower in shades of pink and crimson.

The original orris root iris which can also be known as *Iris* 'Florentina' and *I. germanica*, just to be confusing. The root (which smells of violets) was dried and ground up and used as a fixative for perfume and potpourri by the Greeks and Romans, and as a hair powder and dry shampoo.

IRIS
(Iris flavescens 'Florentina')

IRIS
(Iris germanica)

YELLOW IRIS
(Iris pseudacorus)

This hardy bearded intermediate pale blue-white iris was the medieval emblem for the city of Florence. Irises like to have their tubers exposed to full sun – in parts of France they are planted in a strip at the apex of roofs, making a shaggy cockade of colour in May. All irises need sun, and prefer a neutral soil. Divide and plant rhizomes in late June and early July, or early September, in good composted soil, with all the roots lined up towards the south for maximum sun-ripening. Position the top of the rhizome just proud of the soil, cut the leaves back to half, and keep moist until they are established.

Another May-flowering version of the hardy bearded intermediate iris, also known as the blue flag, and the London flag. It grows 2-3 ft (60–90 cm) tall from tuberous rhizomes, with fragrant purple and white flowers and glaucous evergreen sword-shaped leaves.

A tall, hardy, water-loving deciduous perennial iris, which grows happily at the edge of streams, ponds and lakes. It will also grow in the border, but only half as tall. It flowers in late May to early June. Plant in full sun in March/April or August/September in water up to 18 in (45 cm) deep. Divide the roots while the plant is growing strongly. You can grow it from seed sown in March/April in partial shade, and plant out in September.

HENBANE
(Hyoscyamus niger)

MADDER
(Rubia tinctorum)

MARIGOLD
(Calendula officinalis)

All parts of this plant are poisonous to animals and humans. It grows up to 3 ft (1 m) tall, and produces yellow flowers veined with purple from June until August. The light green leaves are hairy and sticky. Fortunately the plant is not common, and is best avoided.

A straggling plant, with 3 ft (1 m) stems, bearing small yellow flowers which become black berries. It can be grown from seed, is happy on well-drained chalky soil, and naturalizes in hedges and wasteland. The ripened and mature roots are used for dyeing, and for centuries used to be mixed with a powerful array of antisocial ingredients – rancid fat and cowpats being two of the more acceptable.

Sow the seed in situ in late spring in full sun, where it will grow 24 in (60 cm) tall and produce a succession of bright yellow or orange single or double flowers from May until the onset of winter. It will continue to self-seed with no further assistance. This cheerful and amenable plant thrives in poor soil and is happy to be completely neglected. Pinch out the growing tip to make a bushy plant.

FEVERFEW
(Tanecetum parthenium)

SWEET PEA
(Lathyrus odoratus)

LILY
(Lilium regale)

A short-lived bushy perennial usually grown as an annual, producing a myriad white daisy-like flowers with golden centres from July to September. Grown from seed sown in autumn, it will flower the following year. It is happiest in well-drained soil and full sun. Pinching out the first flower buds will encourage the plant to bush out.

A much-loved hardy annual, that will grow up supports to 10 ft (3.5 m) tall in a single summer, and produce pink, mauve, white and purple fragrant butterfly flowers from June to September. Sow the seeds in September or March, harden off out of doors, and plant out in April or May. Mice are extremely partial to the plants, so you might wish to take evasive action. Sweet peas enjoy lots of organic matter under-root, and they are often sown in a trench of manured or composted soil. Pinch out the tips of the plants when they have reached 4 in (10 cm). Dead-head or pick the flowers, and feed with liquid manure every week.

This produces intensely sweet-scented clusters of flushed white bell-flowers in July. It grows to 4–6 ft (1.25–2 m) tall from stem-rooting bulbs which should be planted at a depth of 6–9 in (15–23 cm) in full sun and ordinary soil. The bulbs increase by themselves. Plant them in autumn with plenty of well-rotted manure or compost, leavened with grit or sand if the soil is heavy. Water frequently during the growing season and feed with a liquid manure. Split the clumps of bulbs every few years.

ROSE
(Rosa x alba)

APOTHECARY'S ROSE
(Rosa gallica officinalis)

HOLY ROSE OF ABYSSINIA
(Rosa moschata)

An ancient and particularly fragrant rose which is still grown in Bulgaria for attar. It grows into a large rounded bush up to 6 ft (2 m) high and round, with arching braches and grey-green leaves and bears clusters of small, white, sweetly scented flowers which become bright red oblong hips in autumn. Mulch with well-rotted manure every other year and feed with organic fertilizer and foliar feeds in June and July. It is happy to be trained onto espaliers or onto trellis.

Forms a handsome spreading bush up to 3 ft (2 m) tall, bearing loose semi-double fragrant cerise-red flowers in generous clusters. It was bought to France from Damascus in the 13th century and is a great survivor which flourishes even in poorer soils. *Rosa mundi* is an ebullient striped version with crimson and white flowers and like *Rosa gallica*, produces large scarlet hips in autumn.

A damask rose originally grown in ancient Egypt and in churchyards and monasteries. It grows into a rounded spreading bush up to 5 ft (1.5 m) tall, scattered with clusters of open shell-pink flowers and a tuft of golden stamens.

BOUQUET OF MIXED ROSES
(Rosa gallica; Rosa rugosa)

SCABIOUS
(Scabiosa)

PINKS
(Dianthus caryophyllus)

A fragrant bouquet of gallicas and rugosas bunched in just such a salt-glazed jar as might have graced any medieval table. These ancient roses are easy to grow and unfussy about their soil and situation, but they tend to take over, and usually flower in one glorious burst.

Scabious still grows wild on roadsides and its sky-blue pincushions are scattered on grass verges at midsummer. *Scabiosa atropurpurea* is the variety whose seeds grow freely in the garden, and it comes in a range of colours – purples, reds, pinks, mauves, white and blue. Sow the seeds where they are to flower in March/April or September, and dead-head to prolong the flowering season. It likes an open sunny site.

This 9 in (23 cm) tall plant has grey-green spiky foliage, and tall stems bearing purple, clove-scented flowers in July. Sow the seeds in mid-April and plant out in their eventual flowering site when they have become good bushy plants. They like sharp drainage, lots of sun, well-rotted manure to start them off, and a limy soil.

MULLEIN
(Verbascum thapsus)

Mullein is a biennial which is partial to full sun and rich, gritty, well-drained soil. The stately spires of yellow flowers rise up to 7 ft (2.25 m) tall from June to August, from rosettes of grey-green felted leaves, Sow seeds in April, and plant out in September where they are to flower. They self-seed in the most unlikely and inhospitable places – walls, between paving slabs and the edges of gravel paths are favourites.

MEADOWSWEET
(Filipendula ulmaria)

Meadows and damp woodland are filled with the high white foam of meadowsweet flowers from June to August – it grows abundantly in the wild by ditches and along stream banks. It does well in full sun or semi-shade, and can be increased by root division in spring, or by sowing collected seed in autumn or spring where it is to flower – they may take three years to do so. Mulch in spring, and cut down the plants in October.

LILY OF THE VALLEY
(Convallaria majalis)

A sweetly scented perennial which grows well in moist, chalky, deciduous woodland soil or semi-shade. The roots must be planted just after division in autumn, where the plant is to flower. Lily of the valley grows 6–8 in (15–20 cm) tall and spreads, producing wands of delicious white bell-flowers in April and May. It will grow from seed, but this is a project for the patient, as the plant takes three years to flower.

LOVE-IN-A-MIST
(Nigella damascena)

ST JOHN'S WORT
(Hypericum perforatum)

CORNCOCKLE
(Agrostemma githago)

An enchanting hardy annual, whose tall sky-blue flowers beam from a delicate ruff of feathery green bracts throughout June, July and August, and then produce filigree seed-heads. Deadhead until the end of the flowering season to extend it and encourage larger flowers. They like sunshine and ordinary soil, and will self-seed if left to their own devices. Sow seeds in the flowering site in March.

Used in the Middle Ages for protection against witchcraft, and to heal deep sword cuts, St John's Wort is now valued as an anti-depressant as well. It grows 1–3 ft (30 cm–1 m) tall in limy soils, favouring woodland, grassland and hedgerows. Grow from cuttings or root division, and plant in fertile, well-drained garden soil.

Once upon a time the corn cockle – possibly the same plant as the Biblical tares – was the curse of arable farmers. Now, partly due to their efforts in getting rid of it, it is exceedingly rare. It has reddish-purple flowers and grows in arable fields and roadsides.

ELECAMPANE
(Inula helenium)

A tall – 40 in (75 cm) – eyecatching perennial, it grows well in moist, rich soil, in sun or semi-shade, producing large bright yellow summer flowers. It can be grown very easily from spring-sown seed, and will seed itself profusely, whether you want it or not – it can also be increased by autumn root division.

CANTERBURY BELLS
(Campanula)

White, blue, pink or purple bell-shaped flowers are produced on this somewhat untidy tall biennial from May to July. They are equally happy in sun or partial shade, and enjoy well-drained fertile soil. Seeds should be sown in March/April or October. Plant out the following spring or autumn, when the plants are large enough.

MARTAGON LILY
(Lilium martagon)

Easily grown, martagon lilies are happy in semi-shaded woodland. The recurved rosy purple spotted flowers (which are unpleasantly scented) nod on 5 ft (1.5 m) tall spires in July. Unlike many lilies, martagons can contend with limy soils. They can be grown from seed, planted in September and October, or can be increased by scales taken from the bulbs at the same time. Plant the bulbs 4 in (10 cm) deep and 9 in (23 cm) apart.

RUE
(Ruta graveolens)

A perennial sub-shrub with strongly aromatic glaucous ferny foliage and small, insignificant yellow flowers. It will grow up to 3 ft (1 m) tall, and enjoys well-drained chalky soil and lots of sun. It can be grown from seed sown in late spring, or from cuttings taken in early summer. Trim back to old wood in April to keep the plant bushy.

WHITE BRYONY
(Bryonia dioica)

White bryony can grow up host plants in hedgerows, up to 30 ft (10 m) tall. It has hairy, deeply lobed leaves, and produces five-petalled greenish-yellow flowers in June and July, some of which (only on the female plants) become poisonous red berries in September; the roots are also poisonous.

MARROW FLOWER
(Cucurbita)

Marrows and courgettes are the fruit of large, sprawling annuals, with handsome yellow trumpet flowers. They like warmth, well-drained, rich soil, and may need a 4 ft (1.25 m) square site. They can be sown under glass in early spring, and planted out after the danger of frost, or they can be sown in situ, with protection against slugs. They like lots of water and liquid feed when the fruit is developing.

AGRIMONY
(Agrimonia eupatoria)

TANSY
(Tanacetum vulgare)

HOLLYHOCK
(Althaea rosea)

Agrimony is a widespread perennial, whose starry little yellow flowers enliven roadsides and hedgerows from high summer to early autumn, followed by hooked seedheads. The flowers have an apricot scent and attract bees and other insects. It will grow 24 in (60 cm) tall. Sow seed in late summer or early autumn in well-drained soil.

An insect repellant strewing herb, also used for dyeing, tansy is a hardy perennial which grows up to 4 ft (1.25 m) tall and spreads generously in sun or semi-shade, preferring a well-drained loam. It has rich green feathery leaves, and small, bright yellow, button-like flowers from mid-summer onwards. Propagate by dividing the roots in spring or autumn.

One of the most splendid of cottage garden flowers, the spires of pink hollyhock flowers reach 9 ft (3 m) when grown as a biennial, and half that when grown as an annual, rising from large, ragged, light green leaves. Ideal conditions are a sheltered site, and good rich soil with plenty of well-rotted manure or compost. Sow seed out of doors in June or July and plant where they are to flower in autumn. Keep well watered at all stages of growth.

PURPLE LOOSESTRIFE
(Lythrum salicaria)

A stately plant that colonizes waterside sites by slow-flowing rivers, lakes and ponds. It grows up to 5 ft (1.5 m) tall and flowers with feathery purple spires from June to September. Likes a shady damp position by water, but adapts happily to ordinary garden conditions. Propagate by root division in October or April.

JACOB'S LADDER
(Polemonium caeruleum)

Summer-flowering perennial, happy in full sun and fertile, well-drained soil. It grows 24 in (60 cm) tall, with blue flowers, and is apt to take over if it gets a chance. It is easy to propagate by division in spring, or seed in autumn.

LAVENDER
(Lavandula spica)

Familiar grey-leaved bushy perennial shrub, which adapts uncomplainingly to a wide variety of garden uses – formally clipped or loose and romantic. It bears mauve flowering spikes from July to September. Plant between September and March in well-drained gritty soil, in full sun. Propagate by cuttings taken in August, and planted out the following spring. Cut established plants and lavender hedges hard back in early April to encourage bushiness.

HELLEBORE
(Helleborus)

HOLLY
(Ilex aquifolium)

IVY
(Hedera helix)

An evergreen plant flowering from December to March, making it particularly desirable at a lean time of year. The Christmas rose (*Helleborus niger*) is the true winter flowerer producing lobed leaves and white flowers with golden anthers. Plant in October in good rich moist soil, in light shade, and leave undisturbed. To propagate, sow seeds in summer when ripe, and plant out the following autumn. It will take several years to flower. The Lenten rose (*Helleborus orientalis*) which flowers later in the year produces a variety of different coloured flowers in crimson, purple, pink and white.

An extremely variable species, the most familiar dark, glossy evergreen version of which adorns front doors and mantelpieces at Christmas. Holly has tiny greenish flowers in April or May, which eventually become bright scarlet berries if there are male and female trees together. Hollies do well in sun or shade and a moist loamy soil. They make good hedges and screens and survive city life very successfully. Plant in spring or autumn, and do not allow to dry out. The berries are poisonous.

A hardy evergreen climber which can reach 100 ft (30 m) becoming self-supporting and tree-like at a certain height. It bears greenish-yellow flowers in October and purple-black berries in spring. Ivy may survive for 100 years, growing a hefty stem as broad as a tree-trunk. It does well in all positions and all circumstances, grows and spreads all too easily from aerial roots and layers. Cuttings root very easily, and it can be planted at any time, though from September to March is likely to give it a good start with plenty of moisture.

MISTLETOE
(Viscum album)

GLOBE ARTICHOKE
(Cynara cardunculus Scolymus Group)

SNOWDROP
(Galanthus nivalis)

A long-lived parasitic hardy evergreen shrub 3 ft (1 m) in diameter, which grows in great clusters on apple and poplar trees, and is an essential and mystery-shrouded element of winter celebrations. It can be propagated by pressing ripe berries into a crevice on the underside of a tree branch – birds perform this service in the wild. The plants – which are either male or female – take seven years to fruit. Minute wind-pollinated flowers open in March, followed by the sticky white berries which are particularly appreciated by mistle thrushes.

Handsome perennial grey-leaved thistle (whose immature flowers are what you eat), which can grow 6 ft (2 m) tall and exuberantly broad and looks perfectly at home among herbaceous flowers. In a mild winter the spiky leaves may still be visible. It likes a sheltered sunny planting position in a well-drained sandy loam and ought to have frost protection in winter. You can easily grow artichokes from suckers taken from existing plants, or you can sow seed in spring and plant out the following year.

Snowdrops take a while to get going, but once established will spread and can be increased very easily by dividing clumps as soon as flowering is over. They flower from January onwards. They respond well to good rich soil and partial shade, particularly under deciduous trees. They need to keep moist. Seeds take five years to reach flowering size – scatter them where they are to flower as soon as they are ripe.

Bibliography

Arano, Luisa Cogliati *The Medieval Health Handbook Tacuinum Sanitatis* (George Braziller, 1976).

Burne, John (ed.) *Chronicle of the World* (Thames & Hudson, 1964).

Buchman, Dian Dincin *Feed Your Face* (Duckworth, 1973).

Cannon, John and Margaret *Plant Dyes and Dyeing* (The Herbert Press, 1994).

Conway, David *The Magic of Herbs* (Jonathan Cape, 1973).

Christian, Roy *Old English Customs* (Country Life Ltd, 1966).

Cosman, Madeleine Pelner *Medieval Holidays and Festivals* (Piatkus, 1984).

Davies, R. T. *Medieval English Lyrics* (Faber & Faber, 1963).

Griggs, Barbara *Green Pharmacy* (Robert Hale, 1981).

Grigson, Geoffrey *The Englishman's Flora* (Helicon, 1996).

Grun, Bernard *The Timetables of History* (Touchstone, 1991).

Halliday, F E *An Illustrated Cultural History of England* (Book Club Associates, 1972).

Harvey, John *Medieval Gardens* (Batsford, 1981).

Hatfield, Audrey Wynne *A Herb for Every Ill* (J M Dent, 1973).

Hibbert, Christopher *The English: A Social History* (Paladin, 1987).

Hobhouse, Penelope *Antique Flowers* (Conran Octopus, 1988).

Hobhouse, Penelope *Plants in Garden History* (Pavilion 1992).

Hyams, Edward *A History of Gardens and Gardening* (Dent, 1971).

Landsberg, Sylvia *The Medieval Garden* (British Museum Press).

Mabey, Richard *Food for Free* (Collins, 1972).

Mabey, Richard *Flora Britannica* (Sinclair-Stevenson, 1996).

McLean Teresa *Medieval English Flowers* (Barrie & Jenkins, 1989).

Minter, Sue *The Healing Garden* (Headline, 1993).

Nahmad, Claire *Garden Spells* (Pavilion, 1994).

Paterson, Allen *Herbs in the Garden* (J. M. Dent, 1985).

Rhode, Eleanour Sinclair *The Old English Herbals* (Minerva, 1974).

Sanecki, Kay N. *History of the English Herb Garden* (Ward Lock, 1992).

Shuel, Brian *Guide to Traditional Customs of Britain* (Webb & Bower, 1985).

Thurstan, Viletta *The Use of Vegetable Dyes* (Reeves-Dryad Press, 1977).

Van Zuylen, Gabrielle *The Garden Visions of Paradise* (Thames & Hudson, 1987).

Vickery, Roy *A Dictionary of Plant Lore* (Oxford University Press, 1995).

Costume through the Ages (Thames & Hudson, 1964).

Addresses of gardens to visit

For inspiring contemporary interpretations of the medieval garden, the following gardens are well worth visiting. More extensive details on each are given in the chapter on medieval garden design (pages 120–127), and if you are planning a trip, do make sure you telephone beforehand – the opening times can be bafflingly erratic.

ENGLAND

Queen Eleanor's Garden

Great Hall

The Castle

Winchester

Hampshire

Tel: 01962 846476

FRANCE

Fontevraud Abbey

Centre Culturel de L'Ouest

Abbaye Royale de Fontevraud

49590

Tel: + 33 2 41 51 73 52

Le Jardin Carolingien

Service des Espaces Vers

Melle

Deux Sèvres

79500

Tel: +33 5 49 29 19 54

Les Jardins du Prieure Notre Dame d'Orsan

Lieu dit Orsan

18170 Maisonnais

Tel: +33 2 48 56 27 50

GERMANY

Bebenhausen Abbey

Das Münster (Minster)

Insel Reichenau

Bodensee (Lake Konstanz)

Tel: +49 70 7 16 021 80

WALES

Sir Roger Vaughan's Garden

Tretower Court

Tretower

Crickhowell

Powys

Tel: 01874 730279

Acknowledgements

The work in this book would not have been possible without the painstaking research of my wife Maggie, and the dedication of my daughter Sarah. I also owe a great debt to Miranda Innes, whose style and humour are woven into the text. I would also like to thank Kate Cambell of Eye Abbey in Suffolk for getting me started on it.

With special thanks to:
Angel Flower – Islington; David Austin and his daughter Clare for their help with roses, peonies and irises; Candace Bahouth for inspiration; Elspeth Barker for her Rose Tresoir; Belinda Coote Fabrics, London; Dr Frances Feast for conducting me through Germany; Christine and Trevor Forecast of Congham Hall Country House Hotel in Norfolk for letting me plunder their herb garden and also David Roberts, their gardener; Jenny de Gex for help with research; Annie Huntingdon; John and Leslie Jenkins at Wollerton Old Hall, Shropshire; Anthony Lyman Dixon of Arne Herbs for scholarly advice; Phillip Norman at the Tradescant Museum of Garden History; Mr. Peacock at Kinsfield Conservation for the wild flower afternoon; David Root at Kelways; Watts and Co. Fabric at Chelsea Harbour; Robert and Margaret Weston and their children: Fay, Ella and William for making daisy chains. Stephen Weeks and Kathleen Bull at Penhow Castle, Gwent; Susan and Kevin White of Hexham Herbs, Northumberland; Jackie Cuthill at Queen Eleanor's garden, Winchester; Francesca Kay at Sir Roger Vaughan's Garden, Tretower Court, Powys; Chris Zeuner at the Bayleaf and Downland Museum, Sussex; The administrator at the Carolingien Gardens, Melle, France; Monsieur Robert Carvallo, Chateau de Villandry, France; Sonia Lessaut and Patrice Taretsella for giving me so much assistance at their wonderful medieval reconstruction, The Jardin du Prieure de Notre Dame d'Orsan; the administrator, Fontevraud Abbey, France; the administrator, Bebenhausen Abbey near Stuttgart, Germany; Walfraud and Siegfried Haas, Eizach, Germany; Lynn Raynor, the Herb Garden, Hardstofd, Derbyshire; the curator, Saffron Walden Museum, Essex.

Clay Perry

This book is a testament to the extraordinary talents of the Perry family – Clay who did all the photography, with whom I have had the good fortune to work for a decade or so, and who has never taken a duff picture in his life; Sarah, his daughter, who is a brilliant designer with a fresh and adept touch and more than her fair share of originality; and Maggie who is the powerhouse behind lens, computer, and dinner table. At Kyle Cathie, Candida Hall gave the book shape in the first place, Sophie Bessemer saw it through its gestation, and Alexa Stace marshalled the bits and pieces into a coherent whole. Kyle herself had the vision to come up with the idea and to assemble a fearless team. My personal thanks are due in spades to Dan Pearce, who nagged and cooked, for which thanks were not what he got at the time. And to the RHS Lindley Library, which is a miracle of well-endowed tolerance and in which anyone would be well-advised to browse the works of Geoffrey Grigson and Richard Mabey.

Miranda Innes

Photographic acknowledgements

We are extremely grateful to The Bridgeman Art Library, London for permission to reproduce the following historical images in the book:

Page 1 Floral Decorations, France, Paris
Hours of the Virgin (1515–20)
British Library, London

Page 8 The Labours of the Months, German, 15th century
Victoria and Albert Museum, London

Page 32 A man and a woman removing weeds, apparently thistles, begun prior to 1340 for Geoffrey Luttrell (1276–1345) *Luttrell Psalter* (14th century)
British Library, London

Page 38 Garden of Paradise by Master Oberrheinischer
Stadelsches Kunstinstitut, Frankfurt-am-Main

Page 49 The lover attains the rose, illuminated by the Master of the Prayer Books of c1500, Bruges, *Roman de la Rose* (c1487–1495)
British Library, London

Page 59 Lover in the Garden written by Pierre Sala
Emblemes et Devises d'Amour (early 16th century)
British Library, London

Page 63 A hundred ballads of a lady and her lover, Parisian copy, c141015
Works of Christine de Pisan (c1364–1430)
British Library, London

Page 68 St George and the Dragon (Use of Rome) Flemish *Book of Hours*, probably Bruges (c1500–1505)
Fitzwilliam Museum, University of Cambridge

Page 74 La Vie Seigneuriale-Embrodiery – French 16th century Tapestry
Musée Cluny, Paris
Giraudon

Page 87 April: courtly figure is the castle grounds by the Limbourg brothers
Très Riches Heures du Duc de Berry (early 15th century)
Giraudon

Page 88 The virgin and child with angels in a garden from *Horae B. Mariae Virginis* 15th century
British Library, London

Page 90-91 Garden scene, the lover and dame Oyeuse without, illuminated by the Master of the Prayer Books of c1500, Bruges
Roman de la Rose (c1487–1495)
British Library, London

Page 99 Emilia in her garden
Hours of the Duke of Burgundy (1454–1455)
Osterreichische Nationalbibliothek, Vienna

We are also grateful to the Bodleian Library, Oxford for permission to reproduce the following historical images in the book:

Page 10 Border detail (MS Douce FF59)

Page 112 Detail from Pliny's *Historia Naturalis* Book XXI (MS Douce 310)

For information on the range of fine stationery items based on the photographs in this book, contact:
Chapter and Verse, 96 High Street, Linton, Cambridge CB1 6JT.
Telephone 01223 890 717, Fax 01223 894 137

Index